Tho

H

The Voice of the Martyrs

PO Box 117, Port Credit
Mississauga, Ontario L5G 4L5
Phone: 1.888.298.6423
Fax: 905.670.0246
E-mail: thevoice@persecution.net
Website: www.persecution.net

World Evangelical Alliance

International Institute for Religious Freedom

IIRF

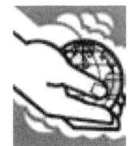

The WEA Global Issues Series

Editors:

Geoff Tunnicliffe,
International Director, World Evangelical Alliance

Thomas Schirrmacher,
Director, International Institute for Religious Liberty and
Speaker for Human Rights of the World Evangelical Alliance

Volumes:

"The WEA Global Issues Series is designed to provide thoughtful
and practical insights from an Evangelical Christian perspective into
some of the greatest challenges we face in the world.
I trust you will find this volume enriching and helpful in your Kingdom service."

Dr. Geoff Tunnicliffe, International Director, World Evangelical Alliance

Thomas K. Johnson

Human Rights:

A Primer for Christians

The WEA Global Issues Series
Volume 1

Verlag für Kultur und Wissenschaft
Culture and Science Publ.
Thomas Schirrmacher
Bonn 2008

World Evangelical Alliance
Suite 1153, 13351 Commerce Parkway
Richmond, BC. V6V 2X7 Canada
Phone +1 / 604-214-8620
Fax +1 / 604-214-8621
www.worldevangelicals.org

*While this volume does not represent an "official" position of the World Evangelical
Alliance we are distributing it to promote further serious study and reflection.*

International Institute for Religious Freedom
of the World Evangelical Alliance
www.iirf.eu / info@iirf.eu

Friedrichstr. 38	PO Box 535	32, Ebenezer Place
2nd Floor	Edgemead 7407	Dehiwela
53111 Bonn	Cape Town	(Colombo)
Germany	South Africa	Sri Lanka

© Copyright 2008 by
Verlag für Kultur und Wissenschaft
(Culture and Science Publ.)
Prof. Dr. Thomas Schirrmacher
Friedrichstraße 38, D-53111 Bonn
Fax +49 / 228 / 9650389
www.vkwonline.de / info@vkwonline.de

ISBN 978-3-938116-61-6 / ISSN 1867-7320

Printed in Germany
Umschlaggestaltung und Gesamtherstellung:
BoD Verlagsservice Beese, Friedensallee 44, 22765 Hamburg
www.rvbeese.de / info@rvbeese.de

Verlagsauslieferung:
Hänssler Verlag / IC-Medienhaus
D-71087 Holzgerlingen, Tel. 07031/7414-177 Fax -119
www.haenssler.de / www.icmedienhaus.de

Privatkunden:
www.genialebuecher.de

The WEA Global Issues Series is sponsored by:

Gebende Hände gGmbH / Giving Hands International
Adenauerallee 11 • D-53111 Bonn • www.giving-hands.de

Martin Bucer Seminar
European Theological School and Research Institutes
Bonn – Zurich – Innsbruck – Prag – Istanbul
www.bucer.eu

CONTENT

FOREWORD

Tom Johnson has taught in several countries of Europe and Asia. He has simultaneously been an evangelical pastor and missionary and a professor of philosophy at secular universities, e.g., in Minsk (Belarus) and in Prague (Czech Republic).

In that my wife and I both have secular academic careers and at the same time have been outspoken evangelicals and missionaries – I am still teaching both world missions in our school and sociology of religion at a state university – I love friends who live on both sides and know both sides by heart, the world and its battles and problems, as well as the beloved church of Jesus Christ, proclaiming the gospel to all the peoples and all of society.

Tom and I both teach ethics and apologetics at our school, the Martin Bucer European School of Theology and Research Institutes, with study centers in several European countries as far away as Istanbul and Ankara in Turkey. But we have not only been engaged in hours and years of debate and developing an evangelical theology which interacts with all problems worldwide while staying truthful to Christ and his Word; we have also been active putting faith into practice in mutual projects, whether it has been helping Romas in Eastern Europe obtain education, testifying to the Minister of Social Affairs in the Czech Republic on the family and how the State can support it, or building up our branch in Turkey.

When we started the International Institute for Religious Freedom, Tom Johnson became the expert on the philosophical and theological foundation of human rights underlying any engagement for human rights, including religious freedom. And thus it was beyond discussion that Tom must write this book for us!

Is the topic ‚Human Rights' just an evangelical obsession because we follow the world and our times – the ‚Zeitgeist,' as we Germans say – more than we follow the Bible – against the clear command of Paul in Romans 12:2? Do we just feel good fighting for human rights because everybody does it and nearly everybody loves us for doing so? Or is there more to it for us as Christians and as Evangelicals?

Are there paths between the biblical message and the topic of human rights, which somehow are the only ethical rules, that hold the major part of the world together in the midst of prevalent relativism?

And if we can justify our being engaged in the cause of human rights from our faith, the question is: Where can we accept what the world says about human rights, and where do we have to offer and testify to our specific Christian and biblical point of view? And how can we assure that this is not only just a Western Christian point of view but something that complements the fact that Christianity has its center in Asia, Africa, and Latin America today, not just in numbers but also with regard to thinkers and theologians who are engaged in the social problems of their continents?

Thomas Schirrmacher

Speaker on Human Rights of the World Evangelical Alliance

Director of the International Institute for Religious Freedom of the World Evangelical Alliance

GRATITUDE

It is always right to give thanks to the many people whom God uses to help us throughout our lives. I cannot do that adequately, but I can mention a few people who helped with this little book. My good friend Prof. Thomas Schirrmacher got me started. Ruth Baldwin and Russ Johnson worked on almost every page in one way or another. Esther Waldrop, Nancy Montgomery, and Janice Gibson gave me valuable comments and corrections. Dr. Daryl McCarthy provided quick, accurate help finding a crucial quotation and source. Giving Hands of Germany provided needed financial assistance. There are four authors whose books have especially helped me try to think before God; they are Helmut Thielicke, C. S. Lewis, George W. Forell, and Francis A. Schaeffer. My wonderful wife, Leslie P. Johnson, has prayed diligently for this project, in spite of her other major responsibilities, because she is deeply convinced that believers can do much better in talking about and defending human rights. Thanks to these people. *Soli Deo Gloria.*

WHY TALK ABOUT HUMAN RIGHTS?

The Shocking Reality of Our World

Dead bodies. Many bodies, naked, emaciated, thrown like garbage against the side of a building. A few survivors, skinny, disoriented, standing, staring. More bodies, scattered here and there. Another pile of naked, skeleton-sized bodies, thrown against a wall. The naïve, arrogant young man who walked into the concentration camp at Dachau was confronted with photographs taken decades before, and his comfortable, secure world went tumbling. Two or three days of shock, too much pain to talk. Then many years of thinking and reading: What happened? Why did we do this to each other? What is wrong with our societies? What is wrong with us? Does it help to scream, "Never again!"?

Then he learns that the Holocaust was not the only holocaust. The many millions who died in the Nazi terror represent many, many other millions who have been sent to horrible deaths for completely irrational reasons.[1] The inhumanity of man toward

---

[1] After going to Rwanda to lead the U.N. genocide investigation in 1994, attorney Gary Haugen began a painful process of reflection on the human condition. After describing the human will to power he commented, "The outcome in the twentieth century could be described in various ways, but I would just call it an open-mouthed grave: an entire generation of European youth composting the World War I battlefields of Verdun and Somme, Hitler's six million Jews, Stalin's twenty million Soviet citizens, Mao's tens of millions of political enemies and peasant famine victims, Pol Pot's two million Cambodians, the Interhamwe's million Tutsi Rwandans, and the millions of lives wasted away during apartheid's forty-year reign." Gary A. Haugen, *Good News about Injustice: A Witness of Courage in a Hurting World* (Downers Grove: InterVarsity Press, 1999) p. 47. Haugen also developed a list of the injustices, really human rights abuses, which he regarded as most prominent at the end of the twentieth century. His list: abusive child labor; abusive police or military; child pornography; child prostitution; corrupt seizure or extortion of land; detention or disappearance without charge or trial; extortion or withholding of wages; forced adult/teenage prostitution; forced migration; genocide; murder of street

man is so vast it defies belief or description. To compare human brutality with animal violence is truly an insult to most animals, not only because humans are more highly organized in their brutality but also because human brutality rarely benefits anyone in any way. Yet humans typically use one of our distinctive abilities, language and words, as an organic part of our brutality; criminals against humanity frequently use special language and words to describe their mass victims as less than fully human, even attempting to convince their victims it is not wrong to murder them.[2]

Many years later this same young man, by then a critical philosopher, privately challenged a God-fearing anti-communist Russian dissident intellectual when the Russian claimed that 100 million people died as a result of Stalin's ideology and violence.[3] The rebuke was kindly but overpowering as this dissident scholar spent part of the evening listing and counting the thousands and millions, including many of his own people, who died because an inhumane worldview had been implemented by an even more inhumane leader. I was that critical philosopher; I asked him to stop counting somewhere past 70 million dead because of Stalin; I could bear no more.[4] Should we scream in despair? Or might it be possible to scream in hope?

---

children; organized political intimidation; organized racial violence; public justice corruption; state, rebel, or paramilitary terrorism; state-supported discrimination or abuse of ethnic minorities; state-sponsored religious persecution; and state sponsored torture. See pages 41 and 42. Some will want to add widespread abortion to his list of injustices.

[2] The Nazis often described the Jews and the other victims of the concentration camps with words that dehumanized them, so that killing them did not sound like it was murder. Their favorite words included pests, parasites, spiders, grasshoppers, vampires, bacteria or tuberculosis bacteria, beasts, and leeches, all of which most societies kill for self-protection, unless it happens to be human beings described with these words. A similar tendency frequently occurs during mass murders, genocide, and crimes against humanity. On the Nazi terms, see Thomas Schirrmacher, *Hitlers Kriegsreligion*, (Bonn: VKW, 2007), Vol. 1, pp. 264, 265.

[3] This number is much higher than is reported in most standard history books.

[4] The visit to the Dachau concentration camp occurred in August 1972. The conversation with the anti-communist dissident scholar was in the mid

Reactions Divine and Human

Crimes against humanity are not new, although the twentieth century was shockingly brutal. About 760 B.C. the biblical prophet Amos declared these words to the countries surrounding his land of Israel:

"This is what the Lord says: 'For three sins of Gaza, even for four, I will not turn back my wrath. Because she took captive whole communities and sold them to Edom, I will send fire upon the walls of Gaza that will consume her fortresses ... For three sins of Tyre, even for four, I will not turn back my wrath. Because she sold whole communities of captives to Edom, disregarding a treaty of brotherhood, I will send fire upon the walls of Tyre that will consume her fortresses ... For three sins of Edom, even for four, I will not turn back my wrath. Because he pursued his brother with a sword, stifling all compassion, because his anger raged continually and his fury flamed unchecked, I will send fire upon Teman that will consume the fortresses of Bozrah ... For three sins of Ammon, even for four, I will not turn back my wrath. Because he ripped open the pregnant women of Gilead in order to extend his borders, I will set fire to the walls of Rabbah that will consume her fortresses amid war cries on the day of battle, amid violent winds on a stormy day.'" (Amos 1: selections from verses 6 through 14)[5]

Although crimes against humanity are not new, modern technology may have allowed a series of attempts to totally annihilate an enemy that were more complete and systematic than the attempts made in the time of Amos. Ripping open the pregnant women with a sword is quite inefficient in comparison with the brutal effectiveness of a well-run concentration camp supported by a totalitarian government in the grip of an inhumane ideology. But whether the crime was committed in Amos' time or in our time, the wrath of God is aroused. God sees each of those

---

1990s in Minsk, Belarus; more details have been withheld for his safety. From February 1994 to June 1996 I was a visiting professor of philosophy at the pro-democracy European Humanities University in Minsk, which was started and led by anti-communist dissident intellectuals. In July 2004 it was closed by force at the orders of the Belarusian dictator, who would not tolerate an openly pro-democracy university in his country.

[5] Unless otherwise noted, quotations from the Bible are from the New International Version.

people as the apple of his eye, created in his own image. God is truly moved to anger with actions that destroy other people. And if, like Amos, we have come to know God, we simply must not fail to speak out in defense of the many in our time who may suffer fates something like the neighbors of Amos. Those who know God must speak out in defense of their neighbors who may suffer current or future crimes against the image of God. And talking properly about our neighbors is part of the solution, since sub-human ways of describing people are so often closely tied to crimes against humanity.

The concern for human rights, meaning the proper treatment of people as people because they are people, did not start after the Holocaust. Right now I am sitting in Athens, where about 2,500 years ago, community leaders began some steps toward a more humane form of life in a democracy, while some of the philosophers began asking what it is that gives human beings their unique dignity, a dignity that requires moral respect and legal protection.[6] But it was after the story of the Holocaust was being widely told that many men and women of good will began to write and talk very extensively about human rights, especially the priority of protecting human rights.

It was the late 1940s that saw some of the more important statements and declarations about human rights and their protection, such as the United Nations Universal Human Rights Declaration of 1948. The Holocaust and other war crimes during World War II gave people such a vivid glimpse into the abyss of human depravity that many stepped back in true horror and said there has to be an alternative. Surely, they thought, we do not need to all become nihilists, saying that life is only about the will to power because there is no truth, no meaning, no basis for human dignity, and no distinction between right and wrong.[7]

---

[6] I am sitting on the floor of a cheap hostel. The truly important questions are not always considered in parliaments, elite universities, or the conference rooms of five-star hotels.

[7] After writing these words, I read the interpretation of the cataclysms in Europe in the twentieth century offered by historian Paul Johnson. Before describing the murderous, totalitarian regimes led by Joseph Stalin and Adolph Hitler, Johnson mentions Friedrich Nietzsche: "He saw God not as an invention but as a casualty, and his demise as in some important sense

Surely, they said, we can identify specific things we must do and not do to each other to avoid acting like a Hitler or a Stalin. Some of these went into the new codes of human rights and laws about human rights. This is worthy of applause.

Why Another Book?

Sadly, the new human rights movement has the same weakness seen already 2,500 years ago in the quest for a humane way of life in ancient Greece. The philosophers of ancient Greece, men like Socrates, Plato, Aristotle, and the Stoics, were searching for a way to understand the world and human experience that did not end in despair. In response to writers and lecturers who said all we have are changing opinions about a changing world, without any truth about religion, the universe, or right and wrong, Socrates and his followers began a quest for unchanging truth and objective standards of right and wrong.[8] Their philosophical

---

an historical event, which would have dramatic consequences. He wrote in 1886: 'The greatest event of recent times—that "God is dead", that the belief in the Christian God is no longer tenable—is beginning to cast its first shadows over Europe.' Among the advanced races, the decline and ultimately the collapse of the religious impulse would leave a huge vacuum. The history of modern times is in great part the history of how that vacuum had been filled. Nietzsche rightly perceived that the most likely candidate would be what he called the 'Will to Power', which offered a far more comprehensive and in the end more plausible explanation of human behaviour than either Marx or Freud. In place of religious belief, there would be secular ideology. Those who had once filled the ranks of totalitarian clergy would become totalitarian politicians. And, above all, the Will to Power would produce a new kind of messiah, uninhibited by any religious sanctions whatever, and with an unappeasable appetite for controlling mankind. The end of the old order, with an unguided world adrift in a relativistic universe, was a summons to such gangster-statesmen to emerge." Paul Johnson, *Modern Times: From the Twenties to the Nineties* (New York: HarperCollins, 1991), p. 48. The quotation from Nietzsche is from *The Joyous Science,* which is sometimes translated into English as *The Gay Science,* which appears in various editions and anthologies. Paul Johnson rejected Nietzsche's atheism but thought Nietzsche was right in his assessment of the probable effects of the arising post-Christian secularism in Europe.

[8] I understand the writing of Socrates, Plato, Aristotle, and some of the Stoics as responses to the ideas of the Sophists. A representative Sophist, Protagoras, is known for claiming "man is the measure of all things." This

quest should have fit with the quest by community leaders for a more humane way of life in society. But their philosophical quest was not informed and guided by the biblical picture of human nature: that humans are both carriers of tremendous dignity because they are created in the image of God, while at the same time they are the sons and daughters of Adam and Eve, who are fallen or bent in such a way that we are all capable of great inhumanity. Therefore, the ancient philosophical quest of my Athenian friends was seriously deficient. And, therefore, ancient Greek efforts to find a humane, democratic way of life were also very weak, leaving many in the grip of inhumane slavery.

The widely articulated need for answers that were not provided by Greek philosophy and religion provided part of the open door for the biblical message when it burst forth from Jerusalem after Pentecost and the commissioning of the early church to take the gospel to all people. Many found that the biblical worldview and gospel answered the big questions that had been left unanswered by any other voice in their society; over the course of a few centuries, the biblical message brought hope, comfort, and truth to many, while also changing entire patterns in the society. In addition to a gospel of eternal salvation, the biblical gospel provided culture-changing answers to the big questions of human nature, truth, and ethics. Greco-Roman literature and philosophy gave a clear voice to many of the important questions that arise in human life and experience, but there was a serious lack of answers to those questions. This situation was part of the "appointed time" for the appearance of the biblical gospel and

---

meant that each man is the judge of all truth and goodness in each and every situation. Whether murder, torture, and slavery are good or bad depends on the judgments or opinions of every person in every situation. This type of Sophism was a skeptical (which would mean we cannot know truth for sure) or nihilistic (which would mean there is no truth) reaction to the encounter of multiple cultures in ancient Greece; somewhat similar reactions are seen in some post-modern reactions to the encounter of multiple cultures today. My understanding of ancient thought is guided by Richard Tarnas, *The Passion of the Western Mind: Understanding the Ideas That Have Shaped Our World View* (New York: Ballantine Books, 1991).

worldview within the Greco-Roman world.[9] The biblical message began to bring peace to restless hearts and truth to questioning minds, and something new began: the birth of a new Christian counter-culture that was contributing to the entire surrounding culture to the extent that many things began to change in all sectors of life.

In our day, the new human rights movement may represent another "appointed time" in the providence of God. It is a cry for a more humane way of life, but it is a cry that lacks answers to the big questions about humanness, meaning, salvation, morality, God, and the universe. It lacks a convincing story that explains both human dignity and human depravity. It is an almost global movement that urgently needs the input that can only come from the biblical message, especially the biblical picture of what it means to be a human being. At its core, the human rights movement is a reaction of horror to crimes against humanity, and this is a proper reaction that Christian believers should share and encourage. But the proper concern for human rights demands answers to the big questions about human life and the world, along with a loving critique of unbelieving theories, joined with the contributions of the best ideas about human rights that have arisen in light of the biblical message. Christians should continue to become the people who demonstrate in practice what it means to care for people in a way that builds and contributes

---

[9] This is a reference to Galatians 4:4-5 , "But when the time had fully come, God sent his Son, born of a woman, born under law, to redeem those under law, that we might receive the full rights of sons." The phrase "when the time had fully come" has also been translated "at the fullness of time" or "at the appointed time." Paul's claim seems to be that there was a special element of timing concerning the Incarnation; this implies that there was also a special work of timing by God in regard to when the gospel was sent forth from Jerusalem to the rest of the world. Providentially God had prepared the way for the gospel in many ways; this included having a widely used language (the type of Greek in which the New Testament was written), a system of Roman roads and other means of transport, and a degree of peace and safety because of Roman law enforcement. Part of this preparation of the proper time was the overall condition of Greco-Roman culture in regard to a deep and widespread awareness of many important life questions, combined with a sense that the religions and philosophies of the age had failed to provide adequate answers.

new institutions and practices that lead to flourishing life, the exact opposite of the horrors of a concentration camp.

A Difficult Challenge

Some of what will follow in the coming chapters may be difficult to understand for some readers. One of the reasons for this is that the language of "human rights," which is commonly used today for questions of political ethics, is a foreign language for many Christians. I do not know any places in the Bible that explicitly use the language of "human rights" to describe God's demands in the realm of civic responsibility, and therefore, the language of "human rights" is not always prominent in basic Christian teaching about ethics. But it would be a serious mistake to even suggest that God is not concerned about human rights; do not forget what God said through Amos. And for almost two thousand years Christian moral teaching has been filled with the concern for how we treat other people, even though the specific terminology of human rights has been used very infrequently.[10]

We have to think in terms of learning the language of human rights in order to communicate our grasp of God's expectations in a language that communicates with people today. Think of the way the Bible has been translated and is being translated into many languages. When the Bible is translated into another language, not only does it make the biblical message available to another group of people; it also tends to change, reformulate, and stabilize the language into which the Bible has been translated. Something like this has happened in many languages. A well educated friend from the tiny country of Latvia tells me that the translation of the Bible into his language is what saved his language, which may have less than two million speakers, from extinction. What they regard as proper Latvian today is heavily dependent on the translation choices made by the people who first translated the Bible into the language, but obviously those

---

[10] Because "human rights" is a language of moral discussion, it is possible for people to use this language to make fundamentally unjust claims and to say stupid things. The proper response is not to stop speaking this language; the proper response is to use this language wisely to protect people and to promote public justice.

translators had to start with an existing language that was spoken within certain communities. That existing language was stabilized and reformulated by the translators, who then passed it on to following generations. Even an atheist who speaks or writes the Latvian language properly has been somewhat influenced by the efforts of Christian Bible translators.

Christians should hope to achieve something similar in the realm of human rights discussions. There is an existing international discussion of human rights, and as we will see, some of this discussion is already influenced by things Christians have said and written in the last millennium. By means of translating biblically informed concerns about protecting people into the language of human rights, we may be able to contribute some improvements to this discussion and help communicate God's Word to our generation. But this will require that a significant number of Christians learn to speak the language of human rights in order to reformulate this language and participate effectively in philosophical discussion and political action. This is a large challenge, but it is not a challenge that should cause us to hesitate. Missionaries learn languages to bring the gospel to other cultures; Bible scholars learn biblical languages to teach the Bible more effectively; computer specialists learn computer languages to improve our technology; and many people have to learn all sorts of languages for a wide range of legitimate purposes. Why not learn the language of human rights to try to protect the weakest of our brothers and sisters?

A Simple Summary

It is possible that a few readers may think it is not possible for them to read an entire book about Christian social ethics, especially a book that may become somewhat theoretical at some points. They may feel like they need to drop out of this discussion soon. If you are one of these dear brothers and sisters, please read at least one more paragraph before you leave us.

The Bible tells us that God is very concerned about how people treat other people because he has made all people in his image. He sees an attack on other people as an attack on himself. Therefore, we should do all we can to protect other people. But because of human sin, we and all people have a tendency to destroy other

19

people. One of the results of sin is that people often think of other people as less than truly human and think they themselves do not have any sinful tendencies that need to be restrained. In order to protect other people more effectively, we need to use every opportunity we have to talk about the value of other people because they are created in God's image, while also talking about the need to restrain the sinful tendencies within all people. There are two sides to the biblical view of a person, and both sides must be remembered. We need to demand that bad governments stop using their powers to hurt people when those people are only doing what they think they have to do; we need to demand that our governments use their powers to protect the lives, rights, and freedoms of people, for this is basic to everything a legitimate government does. Life is always a combination of words and actions; therefore, to protect other people we will always need both words and actions. What we say and do to protect the rights of people should always be clearly based on our Christian faith and informed by the Bible, but many people who are not yet Christians may be convinced of much of what we have to say about human nature, whether or not they accept our Christian faith. Our two-sided view of human nature, created in the image of God with a dignity that reflects that of God, with the continual possibility of using our abilities in demonic ways, can significantly contribute to a way of life in society that is much more humane. Because of who people are, they have rights; because of who people are, we have a tendency to destroy each other. This understanding of human nature can contribute decisively to forming healthy cultures and political systems.

The Motivation

Remember Jesus' parable of the Good Samaritan:

> A man was going down from Jerusalem to Jericho, when he fell into the hands of robbers. They stripped him of his clothes, beat him and went away, leaving him half dead. A priest happened to be going down the same road, and when he saw the man, he passed by on the other side. So too, a Levite, when he came to the place and saw him, passed by on the other side. But a Samaritan, as he traveled, came where the man was; and when he saw him, he took pity on him. He went to him and bandaged his wounds, pouring on oil and wine. Then he put the man on his

own donkey, took him to an inn and took care of him. The next day he took out two silver coins and gave them to the innkeeper. "Look after him," he said, "and when I return, I will reimburse you for any extra expense you may have. (Luke 10:30-35)

When you read the story, you probably tell yourself that you should be a little more like the hero of the story, which is probably what Jesus intended. But parables invite us to reflect further. Imagine what the Samaritan might have thought and done in the following days. Riding on his donkey for many hours he might begin to think, "This sort of thing is happening far too often. I really hate seeing people get hurt. I wonder if we can reduce the number of times this happens in the future. What would be needed? We need a police force that will clean those robbers out of that lonely section on the highway and bring them to justice. For that, we will need an honest government and honest judges who will oversee police officers and establish a reliable system of justice. The judges and police officers will need some specific rules to guide their work. And behind this all we need a deeper explanation of *why* we are doing all this, which will also give some guidance about *how* we try to protect people. It has to be very different from the Roman governors. They sometimes kill people just because they say the wrong thing; think of John the Baptist. And the Romans usually seem to think they have "rights" that the rest of us sub-humans do not have; only Romans really have rights, or so they think. Why did I stop to help that man? It was just an intuitive reaction that I felt was right, but when I think about it, I really believe the stories in Genesis, that God created Adam and Eve different from mere animals, in his image. That is why it was so wrong for Cain to murder Abel; that is why it is so different to kill a person than to kill an animal. We cannot change the fact that Adam and Eve sinned and their sinful hearts were given to their children. But maybe, with a lot of thought, planning, and work, we can reduce the number of attacks on the road between Jerusalem and Jericho. I hate seeing people get hurt so often. It is simply wrong to hurt people. The rest of my life might be busy; it looks like there is a lot of work to do."

Reflection on this parable should lead us to thought and action in regard to protecting the rights of our neighbors.[11]

Rights and Justice

Shortly after the time of Amos, the prophet Micah declared, "He has showed you, O man, what is good, and what does the Lord require of you? To act justly, and to love mercy, and to walk humbly with your God." (Micah 6:8) It is important to notice that the moral demands that we have before God are multiple: justice, mercy, and humility.[12] The practice of mercy is compatible with the practice of justice, because God expects both of us, but the two are not exactly the same. It is not wise to reduce mercy to justice or to reduce justice to mercy. Indeed, recognizing the difference between justice and mercy is closely related to the center of the Christian gospel. Because God is just, he had to demand payment for sin in the form of punishment; because he is merciful and loving, he took that punishment on himself when, in the Person of Jesus, he died on the cross as a substitute. The cross is the place where justice and mercy meet; the fact that mercy and justice can meet shows that they are not the same.

In addition to distinguishing justice from mercy, we should also not forget that there are other moral principles or rules that we should follow. Humility has already been mentioned. Honesty, courage, loyalty, and patience also quickly come to mind. And it is not wise to talk as if, for example, loyalty or honesty is only a variety of justice or mercy. Loyalty to my wife, children, and broader family fits with being just, honest, and merciful, but it

---

[11] I learned this sort of reflection on the parables from the German preacher Helmut Thielicke. His extensive writing on political ethics was largely motivated by this parable.

[12] At least since the time of Ambrose of Milan (339-397) it has been common for Christians to summarize our social ethics around the two principles of justice and love (also called goodwill, liberality, kindness, or mercy). Ambrose summarized the developing Christian consensus when he wrote, "For the social principle can be analyzed under two heads, *justice* and *goodwill*." *From Irenaeus to Grotius: A Sourcebook in Christian Political Thought,* Oliver O'Donovan and Joan Lockwood O'Donovan, editors, (Grand Rapids: Eerdmans, 1999), p. 84. Humility before God, mentioned by Micah, is not so much a principle of social ethics as it is a key to an honest relationship with God.

seems to confuse matters if I talk about loyalty to family and spouse as being only justice or only love. If I do something that is disloyal to my wife and family, it may also be unloving and unjust, but it is especially disloyal. The disloyalty is probably what makes abandonment of wife and children so unjust and unloving. It is best to keep these different principles clear and distinct in our minds.

This distinction among justice, mercy, and other moral principles is important when discussing human rights. We will avoid a lot of confusion if we keep in mind that human rights are primarily in the realm of justice, not primarily in the realm of mercy or loyalty. When we demand the protection of human rights in society, we are calling on governments, citizens, and all other organizations to practice justice. Some of the human rights codes since the Holocaust have been confused at this point. The authors were usually very sensitive to human need and suffering, but they have often failed to distinguish the demands of justice (protecting human rights) from other important moral demands (such as caring for human needs). From some such codes of rights, one can receive the impression that it is almost as evil for a government to provide slightly inadequate pensions for retirees as it is for a government to send people to concentration camps or to commit genocide. This impression, which is surely not what was intended by such authors, is given whenever adequate pensions are described as a human right. It would be far better to say that the moral principles that relate to retirement pensions are loyalty (between generations) and mercy (to people in need), not primarily human rights, which are a matter of the most fundamental justice. In light of the cross of Jesus, one can see that justice and mercy are both different from each other and related to each other; without the intellectual light given by the cross and the Christian gospel, people tend to confuse or join mercy and justice. Justice protects rights, whereas mercy and love respond to needs.

Nevertheless, there is a vital connection between a concern for human rights and other important moral principles; that connection is how we treat other people. Moral or ethical considerations usually have to do with how we treat other people; our worst actions usually arise from treating other people as objects instead of treating them as people. The enhanced version of the story of the Good Samaritan shows how mercy (concern and action to help a person in need) naturally leads to actions that will promote justice (so more people do not get hurt by criminals). We may even say there is a moral/spiritual continuity from helping people in need to taking legal or political action to protecting the rights of people; to see this point, just think about the story of the Good Samaritan for a time.

Rights, Worldviews, and Religions

There is a complex relationship among the practical protection of human rights, the various religions, the various political ideologies and worldviews, and the biblical view of a person. This complexity arises from the way in which our knowledge of God and our knowledge of human nature interact with each other in a circular manner. Evangelical theology has long recognized and discussed this interaction between our knowledge of God and of human nature. One of the earlier evangelical theologians, John Calvin, wrote, "Nearly all the wisdom we possess, that is to say, true and sound wisdom, consists of two parts: the knowledge of God and of ourselves. But, while joined by many bonds, which one precedes and brings forth the other is not easy to discern."[13] Calvin saw the knowledge of God and the knowledge of human nature as standing in a dynamic, dialectical relation with each other.

Getting to know God should lead to a proper understanding of human nature, in both our dignity and our fallenness, and this knowledge of human nature should lead to a protection of the rights of all people. On the other hand, a sense of human dignity and human fallenness can arise in many ways, including reactions to atrocities and sins, and this can lead people to consider and know the ultimate Source in whose image we are created. Our everyday experience of ourselves, other people, and the world should give us a deep sense of both human dignity and human fallenness, joined with an awareness of God, but this does not always happen. Many times we want to hide from the

---

[13] John Calvin, *Institutes of the Christian Religion,* Book 1, Chapter 1, section 1.

truth, whether it is the truth about God, others, or ourselves; we have been doing this since Adam and Eve played a silly game, trying to hide from the living God behind a bush or tree. Some religions, worldviews, and political ideologies are the expression of the human attempt to hide from God, which leads to an attempt to deny both human dignity and human fallenness; these religions, worldviews, and ideologies sometimes lead to the abuse of human rights, not toward the protection of human rights. Such religions and ideologies tend to help people hide from the truth about themselves, others, and God. Good examples of this problem would be Communism, National Socialism, and some types of radical Islam.

In the context of people hiding from the truth about themselves, others, and God, a bright light can shine when the people who know God also proclaim and act on the truth about human beings. Corrie ten Boom was a Dutch Christian woman who was sent to a Nazi concentration camp because of her family's efforts to protect Jews during the Nazi occupation of the Netherlands during World War II. She survived and was able to tell her story in *The Hiding Place*. The whole book is a testimony of how the biblical worldview and the Nazi worldview lead to entirely different results in how we talk about people and treat people. She recounts an important dialogue she had with a young Nazi officer who was interrogating her. The officer, a lieutenant, was attempting to get ten Boom to tell him more about her group, which was protecting some Jews.

"Your other activities, Miss ten Boom. What would you like to tell me about them?"

"Other activities? Oh, you mean—you want to know about my church for mentally retarded people!" And I plunged into an eager account of my efforts at preaching to the feeble-minded.

The Lieutenant's eyebrows rose higher and higher. "What a waste of time and energy!" he exploded at last. "If you want converts, surely one normal person is worth all the half-wits in the world!"

I stared into the man's intelligent blue-gray eyes; true National-Socialist philosophy I thought, tulip bed or no. And then to my astonishment I heard my own voice saying boldly, "May I tell you the truth, Lieutenant Rahms?"

"This hearing, Miss ten Boom, is predicated on the assumption that you will do me that honor."

"The truth, Sir," I said, swallowing, "is that God's viewpoint is sometimes different from ours—so different that we could not even guess at it unless He had given us a Book which tells us such things."

I knew it was madness to talk this way to a Nazi officer. But he said nothing so I plunged ahead. "In the Bible, I learn that God values us not for our strength or our brains but simply because He has made us. Who knows, in His eyes a half-wit may be worth more than a watchmaker. Or—a lieutenant."

Lieutenant Rahms stood up abruptly. "That will be all for today." He walked swiftly to the door. "Guard!"

I heard footsteps on the gravel path.

"The prisoner will return to her cell."

Following the guard through the long cold corridors, I knew I had made a mistake. I had said too much. I had ruined whatever chance that I had that this man might take an interest in my case.

And yet the following morning it was Lieutenant Rahms himself who unlocked my cell door and escorted me to the hearing. Apparently he did not know of the regulation that forbade prisoners to step on the mat, for he indicated that I was to walk ahead of him down the center of the hall. I avoided the eyes of the guards along the route, guilty as a well-trained dog discovered on the living room sofa.

In the courtyard this time a bright sun was shining. "Today," he said, "we will stay outside. You are pale. You are not getting enough sun."

Gratefully I followed him to the farthest corner of the little yard where the air was still and warm. We settled our backs against the wall. "I could not sleep last night," the lieutenant said, "thinking about that Book where you read such different ideas. What else does it say in there?"

On my closed eyelids the sun glimmered and blazed. "It says," I began slowly, "that a Light has come into this world, so that we need no longer walk in the dark. Is there darkness in your life, Lieutenant?"

There was a very long silence.

"There is great darkness," he said at last. "I cannot bear the work I do here."[14]

Because of their biblical faith and worldview, the ten Boom family sacrificed themselves to protect their Jewish neighbors, whom they saw as created in the image of God. Their knowledge of God led to a knowledge of people as carriers of God's dignity, who must be protected from the results of the fallenness which resides within us. But as is normal in all of life, actions were accompanied by words of explanation. And those words of explanation began to bring Light to other people, even a Nazi officer trained to think of his prisoners as parasites and bacteria, opening a door of repentance for him. The words and actions of the ten Boom family began to give him a knowledge of himself as filled with darkness, breaking through the prison of the Nazi ideology. This led him immediately to a more humane way of treating other people, beginning with ten Boom herself. Oh that a thousand other Nazi officers had spent some time listening to Corrie ten Boom!

Screaming "Never again!" is a good start in our response to the atrocities of our world, but we have to go further. We need a wide range of actions, policies, and legal/political structures that protect people; and we need to say very, very clearly, "God values us not for our strength or our brains but simply because he has made us." Such words cut through the darkness of deceptive ideologies and religions, while also pointing to the real Light. This message brings light and hope to a scream of protest.

There is today a vast human rights movement comprised of a huge number of organizations, often connected with humanitarian aid organizations. Their combined efforts seem to be reducing the number and extent of atrocities around the world, bringing some criminals against humanity to justice, and providing important aid to people in need. This is a very humane and proper reaction to the TV and newspaper pictures of suffering which disturb our peace of mind. This book is intended to support this movement in two ways: 1, to challenge evangelical Christians to be ever more active in working and speaking for human rights;

---

[14] Corrie ten Boom, with John and Elizabeth Sherrill, *The Hiding Place* (Washington Depot: Chosen Books, 1971), pp. 148, 149.

and 2, to challenge those already concerned or active to protect human rights to think more deeply about the moral, religious, and philosophical foundations for their concern. Because of the unity of words and action in human life, some reading and thinking may contribute to protecting people in the image of God.

HUMAN RIGHTS AND THE HUMAN QUEST

Without God?

"'It comes to this,' Tarrou said almost casually: 'What interests me is learning how to become a saint.'

'But you don't believe in God.'

'Exactly! Can one be a saint without God?—that's the problem, in fact the only problem I'm up against today.'"[15]

Albert Camus wrote these memorable lines in his novel *The Plague,* published in 1947, after observing the first half of a century marked by unbelievable brutality: two world wars which cost the lives of so many millions; war crimes of previously unknown magnitude in both Europe and Asia; the Holocaust; and also some knowledge of Stalin's purge of the Soviet Union at the cost of millions of lives. Camus's reactions contributed to the worldwide reactions that led to the international concern for human rights. When Camus wrote these penetrating lines, at least three important matters were pressing on his mind.

First, he was deeply sensitive to human suffering, described so profoundly in all his fiction, which may either be caused by human brutality or allowed to continue because of a lack of human moral sensitivity. The unprecedented cruelty toward people demonstrated by Hitler and Stalin convinced Camus that life is meaningless and forced him to wonder if suicide were the only sensible response to such cruelty and the absurdity of life.[16]

---

[15] Albert Camus, *The Plague* (New York: Modern Library, 1948), p. 229.

[16] Camus began his essay, "The Myth of Sisyphus: An Absurd Reasoning," with the claim, "There is but one truly serious philosophical problem, and that is suicide. Judging whether life is or is not worth living amounts to answering the fundamental question of philosophy." This has the distinct ring of an autobiographical reflection; apparently many committed suicide after coming face-to-face with radical evil in his time. Camus recom-

Second, he was wrestling with Dostoevsky's Dilemma, articulated by Fyodor Dostoevsky's character Dmitry Karamozov in *The Brothers Karamozov,* "If there is no God, then everything is permitted." Camus was an atheist for most of his life, whereas Dostoevsky believed in God. And Camus realized that if God does not exist, then it is very difficult to avoid becoming a nihilist, feeling like and believing that there is no truth, no meaning for life, and no distinction between right and wrong. Indeed, Camus confessed about his writings, "I have only sought for a means to overcome nihilism."[17]

Third, Camus honestly faced some important facts of normal moral experience that seemed to contradict his atheism and the nihilism that easily follows from atheism: deep inside ourselves we feel sympathy for the needs and suffering of other people, joined with a feeling of duty, that we have a moral obligation to other people or for other people, all of which is somehow based on an intuition that humans have a unique dignity and destiny. But if human life is nothing but a cosmic accident, not in any way caused or created by God, why should human suffering bother me any more than the suffering of an insect? And why do I have this strong sense of moral obligation in relation to other people? For these reasons, the hero of Camus's novel decides to try to become a saint without God, struggling to reduce or overcome human suffering. However, this point of view contains so much internal tension that Camus himself could not continue trying to be a saint without God. His awareness of human need, suffering, and our common human moral obligation pushed him to break out of the dilemma and conclude that there must be a God who created human beings with a special dignity and destiny and who somehow stands behind moral obligation. Shortly before his

---

mended the effort to continue to struggle for a humane way of life as a protest against the absurdity of life.

[17] Albert Camus, *L'Éte,* quoted by James Sire, *The Universe Next Door: A Basic Worldview Catalog,* Third Edition (Downers Grove: InterVarsity, 1997), p. 95. My interpretation of Camus and French existentialism is dependent on James Sire and on C. Stephen Evans, *Existentialism: The Philosophy of Despair and the Quest for Hope* (Grand Rapids: Zondervan, 1984).

death in a tragic auto accident, Albert Camus requested Christian baptism.[18]

This dilemma, so eloquently articulated by Dostoevsky and Camus, stands at the heart of the modern human rights movement. Does the extent of evil and suffering tell us to become atheist nihilists and say that there is no God, no meaning, and no distinction between right and wrong? Or is the attempt to try to become a saint without God the right response? Or does the humane response of so many indicate that God exists and that we know him unconsciously as the precondition of our lives? There is a strong internal connection between a practical concern for human rights, really for protecting people, and the quest into which we have all been thrown by the fact of birth. We cannot avoid the big questions: Who are we? What gives human life value? What is this world? Where did it come from? What is wrong with the world? What is wrong with us? Why do we have a sense of moral obligation? Why can we not avoid crying out for justice? Why can we not avoid crying out for mercy? So, I have to ask, What does the existence of the human rights movement tell us about the nature of the universe and ultimate Truth?

A Wide Concern and Big Questions

It would be a serious mistake to think that the quest for human dignity and the concern for human rights are matters only for philosophical novelists like Camus or Dostoevsky. A quick Google search of the internet identifies 77,400,000 items one might read on the subject of human rights.[19] There are millions of other

---

[18] Some of Camus's personal story is told by Howard Mumma, *Albert Camus and the Minister* (Brewster, Massachusetts: Paraclete Press, 2000). Most of what was known about Camus's progress toward accepting the Christian faith could not be told until long after his death, because Howard Mumma was bound by his vows of pastoral confidentiality. This citation of Mumma's book is not an endorsement of the way Mumma demythologized parts of the Bible.

[19] On April 12, 2008. This number was only in English. There are millions of other documents in other languages. On that date Google found 3,190,000 items to read in German and 890,000 documents in the rather small Dutch language. If one only read Dutch, there would enough reading on the subject of human rights to last several lifetimes.

documents on the topic of human dignity. The annual US State Department world report on human rights has grown to more than 5,000 pages published each year; the European Union annual world human rights report is limited to a readable size, about 100 pages, but it is published in 20 languages. The US, the EU, and the UN have budgeted very significant funds for their human rights/human dignity programs; a review of founding documents shows that the US, the EU, and the UN were all started to protect human rights, even though all three have sometimes failed to implement or have even forgotten their central purposes.[20] And the end of Communism in much of central and eastern Europe in the late twentieth century was largely a result of the people of the region asserting their dignity and subjectivity as human beings; this assertion of dignity and subjectivity led to the recognition of basic rights, matters such as freedom of speech, freedom of religion, and freedom of assembly.[21]

Surely all people of good will must rejoice that so many people are investing so much time, energy, and money into the search for human dignity and the attempt to protect human rights. It is surely much better to attempt to become a saint without God than to become a villain or criminal against humanity without God. Almost all of us can see that there is a huge difference between Adolph Hitler, Joseph Stalin, or Pol Pot on the one hand

---

[20] An excellent general account of the human rights movement is Geoffrey Robertson QC, *Crimes against Humanity: The Struggle for Global Justice* (London: Penguin Books, first edition 1999, third edition 2006), 759 pages. Robertson sometimes misinterprets classical natural law theory which was influenced by Christianity. One example is the way in which he mistakenly makes a close connection between natural law ethics and the supposed "Divine Right of Kings," which was used to support inhumane tyranny at times in Western history.

[21] After living in formerly Communist countries for fourteen years, I think that much of what caused the widespread, mostly peaceful revolt against Communism in the late twentieth century was a different conception or perception of what a person is. The Communist authorities largely saw people as objects to be controlled or used; the people experienced themselves as creative subjects who needed freedom of speech, freedom to travel, and freedom of assembly in order to reach their potential. For some, freedom of religion was crucial reason to replace Communism.

and Mother Teresa or Corrie ten Boom on the other hand, and we would prefer to live in a world influenced by the examples of Mother Teresa and Corrie ten Boom. But it would be cowardly to refuse to consider the big questions about life, Truth, and the universe which are raised by atrocities and the irrepressible humane response of attempting to protect human life and rights.

Let me again state my perspective: human atrocities and the responding human rights movements are best understood in the light of the description of life and the world which arises from the Christian Bible. There are several big questions about life and the universe that are raised by human evil and our responses that call for justice and mercy; these questions find the best answers in the biblical message, and the biblical message even explains why we ask these questions. From the time of Adam and Eve, God has been pursuing the sons and daughters of Adam and Eve by means of questions that are somewhat like his question in the Garden of Eden: "Where are you?" Through the acknowledgement of human evil and the responding human rights movement, some ultimate questions require our attention. Why do we have an awareness of a standard for human behavior? What is it about us humans that gives us rights different from those of an insect? Why do we so frequently destroy each other? Is even the "saint without God" really responding to God's moral demand built into the world and human consciousness? The Bible not only gives credible answers to these questions; it also explains why we can hardly avoid asking such questions.

There are at least four big questions that require answers.

1. Why Do We Know the Difference between Good and Evil?

It is common to think that everyone but a psychopath knows there is a difference between good and evil. Even though a philosopher or novelist can easily say that if God does not exist, then everything is permitted, in practice almost all normal people draw back and think that some things are really wrong, while other things are really right.

Many years ago, when I was a nasty young lecturer in philosophy, I played a philosophical trick on a young woman in an

33

ethics class I taught. She wrote a course essay in which she argued brilliantly that all ethical concerns were a matter of taste; just as some people like ice cream while others like candy, some people like one set of actions while others like another set of actions. It clearly followed from her essay that it is equally good to like genocide or to like protecting human rights. My nasty trick was to write on her paper, "Excellent essay; failure." She was quite angry when she came to see me a few days later. "How can you fail me if I wrote an excellent essay?" she almost screamed. I calmly responded, "It tasted good. Ethics is a matter of taste." "But a good paper deserves a good grade!!" she huffed. With a bored glance I responded, "You convinced me. Everything is relative." "BUT THERE ARE RULES!! GOOD PAPERS GET GOOD GRADES!! EVEN PROFESSORS HAVE TO FOLLOW THE RULES!!" And then the light went on in her mind. Her anger at me showed her that she did not really believe the things she had written in her philosophy essay. She really thought (contrary to everything she had written) that we all know a lot about right and wrong and there are real standards of proper behavior that are different from matters of taste. I gave her a good grade for what she learned, but her whole relativistic philosophy of life was broken to pieces. Like most people, she not only believed in a standard of right and wrong (in spite of what she said she believed); she also knew that I knew the same standard of right and wrong. Her denial of a standard of right and wrong was only a fashionable game she was playing. By losing her game, she may have begun to recover her soul.

I wish I could claim that this philosophical trick was my own idea; honesty requires that I say I learned it from C. S. Lewis.[22] This trick shows something important about our moral knowledge; with Lewis, I would claim it also shows something very important about our selves and about the nature of the universe. And these truths about moral knowledge, our selves, and the

---

[22] My trick was inspired by reading the first part of *Mere Christianity*, where Lewis points out that moral conflicts show that our real moral knowledge may be very different from what some say they think. For a better presentation of these ideas, please read the first part of Lewis's book, which is available in various editions in English and also in various other languages.

nature of the universe are best explained by the biblical account of God, the moral law, and human fallenness.

Lewis invited people to notice the structure of any argument between two people. Simply put, I will consistently argue that I have done the right thing while you have done the wrong thing, while you can be expected to argue that you have done the right thing while I have done the wrong thing. Almost never, in any real argument, does anyone say anything like "There is no standard of proper behavior" or "We can't know right and wrong." Both parties to an argument assume that there is a real difference between right and wrong and that we all have reasonably good knowledge of the standard of right and wrong. I was testing this claim of Lewis in the philosophical trick I played on the young woman in my ethics class, and I thought that Lewis's claim passed the test.

Of course, as Lewis knew, many people do not believe there is a moral law (which he also called the natural law or the law of human nature). Some claim that what Lewis and I are calling a moral law is only an instinct or a social custom, but those people have not really thought about their own moral experience or what they are saying. Of course we have instincts, but we are also normally aware of something outside our instincts telling us which instincts we should obey and which we should disobey; that is the moral law.[23] Of course we have social customs, but we are also aware that we can and must evaluate different customs (e.g., should we or should we not practice genocide?) on the basis of some higher standard; that is the moral law.

At this point in the discussion, we all become rather uneasy, for we can hardly avoid the question of where this moral law comes from. Should we conclude that our moral knowledge is based on a real moral law that exists outside our minds? Then consistency will strongly push us to conclude that God exists, that the moral law exists in his mind, and that he has created us in such a way that there is some reflection or image of his law in our minds, even though we sometimes wander in the dark on moral issues. If we do not want to conclude that God really exists, then consis-

---

[23] We may also be aware at times that one of our instincts is either too weak or too strong.

tency will push us to say and think that there is no real difference between good and evil.

For at least a few hundred years, the so-called "Problem of Evil" has been a continuous objection to Christian belief that one encounters in almost every western introduction to philosophy. A classical form of the claim comes from the Scottish philosopher David Hume. He asked, "Is God willing to prevent evil and unable? Then he is not omnipotent. Is he able but not willing? Then he is malevolent. Is he both willing and able? Whence then is evil?"[24] Using arguments like this, many thoughtless people have claimed that the existence of real evil in the world somehow makes belief in God impossible or more difficult. But this is silly. Such people have never considered what would have to follow if God does not exist; they should spend a day or two reading Camus. If God does not exist, we would not be able to say "This is evil" and really mean anything by what we said. For if God does not exist, there is no standard of evaluation to say if something is good or evil; all we could say is that some people like it and others do not like it.

A real evaluation that something is evil depends on having a standard that is beyond the opinions of one person or one group of people. Was the Holocaust evil? Hitler and his friends thought it was good. If you think it was truly evil, you must assume there is a standard outside the differing opinions of people; without thinking about it, you have probably assumed that this standard exists in the mind of God and that the human mind can somehow learn something from the mind of God. Do you think it was truly evil that Stalin caused the deaths of about 100 million people? Stalin and his friends probably thought it was good. In order to disagree in an intelligent manner, you must think there is a standard of right and wrong beyond mere human disagreements which we can know at least in part. In order to say that 100 million murders is evidence of real evil, we all very naturally assume knowledge of a standard or rule of right and wrong which is above our changing opinions. We all assume a certain

---

[24] This discussion occurs in David Hume's *Dialogues Concerning Natural Religion*, which he finished writing in 1776 and which was published posthumously in 1779. It is available in a variety of editions, and excerpts are included in many anthologies of important texts in western philosophy.

amount of moral knowledge which comes from God as part of his moral law built into human consciousness; it is part of being created so that our minds are in the image of God's mind.

The fact that most normal people can recognize the difference between good and evil and call the actions of a Hitler or Stalin truly evil, is, I think, a strong indicator of the existence of God and the truthfulness of the biblical description of human life. For me, the "Problem of Evil" is not how a good and omnipotent God can allow suffering. For me, the real problem of evil is how a real difference between good and evil could both exist and be recognized by us if God did not exist. Our normal recognition of evil, including the massive human rights movement dedicated to reducing evil, is possible only because God exists and we have at least some God-given knowledge of right and wrong.[25]

After thinking deeply about human wickedness, Camus initially recommended becoming saints without God. But then he reconsidered this most basic question. Why not?

2. What Is So Distinctive about Humans That We Have Rights?

The atheist philosopher Bertrand Russell clarified the question very nicely:

> If men developed by such slow stages that there were creatures which we should not know whether to classify as human or not, the question arises: at what stage in evolution did men, or their semi-human ancestors begin to be all equal? ... A resolute equalitarian ... will be forced to regard apes as equals of human

---

[25] It seems to me that there are usually two types of people who are seriously interested in the so-called "Problem of Evil" as a reason to reject Christian belief. The first type of person has been so deeply hurt by human suffering that he or she is continually angry at God; for this person, the Problem of Evil is an expression of anger at God. What better way to tell God how angry you are than to tell him he does not exist? Of course, this emotional reaction shows that people can hardly avoid some knowledge of God. The second type of person uses the Problem of Evil as an intellectual game to avoid an honest confrontation with God; the nature of the game shows that the real problem is the sinful desire to avoid God, not an intellectual problem with Christian belief.

beings. And why stop with apes? I do not see how he is able to resist arguments in favor of Votes for Oysters.[26]

Of course, Russell was totally facetious in his mention of "Votes for Oysters." But what is it about humans that makes us so different that humans have a dignity or rights or a value that oysters do not have? Or that insects do not have? Or that bacteria do not have?[27]

Bertrand Russell was writing at a time in Western culture when many thoughtful people were beginning to realize they did not know what a human being is. At earlier times in Western history, as I interpret that history, most people in Western culture had some ideas about makes us human or what gives humans their distinctive dignity. Many (though not all) people, even if they were not personally Christians, had views about human beings that were heavily influenced by the biblical message. Different people used different terms to describe this distinctive value of human life, whether in terms of humans possessing an immortal soul or having God-given inalienable rights or by talking about the image of God in mankind; all these ways of talking and thinking were heavily influenced by different parts of the Bible.

But in the early twentieth century, this influence of the Bible on Western culture began to disappear. Under the influence of atheistic versions of evolutionary theory, some people began to say there is nothing distinctive about humans that would give us

---

[26] Bertrand Russell, *History of Western Philosophy* (New York: Routledge, 1946), pp. 697-698. Quoted by Howard Taylor, *Human Rights: Its Culture and Moral Confusions* (Edinburgh: Rutherford House, 2004), p. 50.

[27] I read a recent news report about a Swiss government ethics committee that is debating whether or not flowers have an inherent dignity which requires they not be cut. The very fact that this type of discussion occurs probably shows a lack of clarity about the difference in dignity between human life and non-human life. Because it is God's creation, people whose lives and thinking are guided by the Bible should be very responsible in their stewardship of the creation and should want to avoid unneeded cruelty to animals, while we are also very clear that humans have a dignity different from the rest of creation because humans are created in the image of God. Some parts of the environmental movement have lost sight of the distinctive dignity of humans.

special dignity or special rights.[28] Under the influence of behaviorist theories in psychology and the other social sciences, some even talked as if personal decision-making is only a façade.[29] Freud and his followers talked as if humans are only a bundle of instincts, mostly sexual instincts, while the various followers of Nietzsche thought it was the will to power which makes us human. So what makes us human? Does anyone know? Or is there anything that is distinctly human? Is there any difference between a human and anything else in the universe?

Frances Schaeffer talked about a "line of despair" in Western history; after centuries of optimism about finding truth, sometime in the early twentieth century, people in the West began to despair of truth, meaning, morality, and understanding humanness. Bertrand Russell was clearly a man who lived below the line of despair. Like many others, he thought human life was a cosmic accident with no particular significance or value. He wanted a humane way of life, but he had terrible troubles trying to say what it is that makes us human.

I have told a bit of the story of how difficult it is for people in Western culture to say what it is that makes human life so distinctive that humans have rights that insects and oysters do not have. It would be valuable to tell similar stories about how different cultures around the globe are struggling to define

---

[28] For sake of honesty, we must mention that there are some people, including prominent natural scientists, who believe most of evolutionary theory but insist that there is such a prominent difference between humans and non-human animals that one has to think that God specially intervened in the process of evolution to make humans decisively different from anything that came before. See Francis S. Collins, *The Language of God: A Scientist Presents Evidence for Belief* (Free Press, 2006). Every culture has a story of origins which it tells as an alternative to the Genesis creation account; this makes me wonder how much of the evolutionary story is just one more story of origins, written by leading representatives of a natural science-oriented culture.

[29] Here I am especially thinking of the influence of B. F. Skinner. The title of his most important book shows much of what he thought: *Beyond Freedom and Dignity*.

humanness; it is a global question. Is there really a difference between humanity and nature?[30] What is it?

We should be clear about the significance of this question. If there is no difference between killing a million people who are perceived as a threat to my or to our interests and killing a million insects that are a threat to my or to our interests, then there is no basis for a worldwide human rights movement. The entire human rights movement makes sense only on the assumption that there is a real difference between humans and the rest of nature. But what is that difference? Do we have to end in despair? Must we simply say that "it tastes better" to protect humans than to protect insects or bacteria? But then most of the great criminals against humanity thought it somehow pleasant or desirable to kill many human beings.

I do not think we have to despair about clarifying a significant moral difference between humans and other entities. At the very least, most of us have everyday experiences and relationships that almost force us to conclude that human beings are distinct from the rest of the world and somehow special in the world. I like our family dog and even talk to her, but I know directly and certainly that our dog is fundamentally different from my children or my wife. We have direct awareness that humans are distinct and special in the universe. We experience ourselves, including our thoughts, hopes, and anxieties, knowing that other people have similar thoughts, hopes, and anxieties; this leads us very naturally to conclude that we are different from a bird or an insect.[31] And it is easy to start listing some important differences between humans and other animals or objects. People think, talk, create, imagine, have deep relationships, and make value decisions in a way that nothing else does. Our dog has never asked me a theological or philosophical question; my children started asking the big questions about life as soon as they could talk. Part of our humanness surely must be the ability to ask the

---

[30] The way of phrasing these questions, as well as the overview of the problem in Western culture, is partly dependent on Richard Tarnas, *The Passion of the Western Mind*, pp. 326-332.

[31] I think these experiences are God-given and are part of God's general revelation, which will be described further below.

big questions and wonder about the universe; I think we are the only residents of planet earth who do these things.

Such everyday experiences make me think there is good reason to say that humans are distinct in our world, in contradiction with what some think they have learned from Darwin, Skinner, or Freud. We should doubt any academic theory that stands in conflict with the one area of knowledge about which we have inside knowledge, being human. Any religious or philosophical theory about humanness should explain my inside knowledge of what it means to be human; such theories should not ask me to deny my internal and direct knowledge of being human.

The description of humanness given in the Bible is worthy of serious consideration, even by people who are not Christians or Jews. In the opening sections of the Bible we are told:

> Then God said, "Let us make man in our image, in our likeness, and let them rule over the fish of the sea and the birds of the air, over the livestock, over all the earth, and over all the creatures that move along the ground." So God created man in his own image; in the image of God he created him; male and female he created them. God blessed them and said to them, "Be fruitful and increase in number; fill the earth and subdue it. Rule over the fish of the sea and the birds of the air and over every living creature that moves on the ground." Genesis 1:26-28.

It is probably impossible to prove exactly when and how God did this; this is at the very beginning of history, so there were not many reporters around to write articles for their newspapers. But this is not silly nonsense; it is a profound but simple answer to one of our biggest questions: "What are we?" The words "image of God" and "likeness of God" (typical Hebrew poetic parallelism that likes repetition) do not give us a lot of detail, but they do tell us that humans are something like God, the ultimate Ground of the universe. There is something in humans that is analogous to (an image or reflection of) God himself. Can anything deeper be said? This description of human life would not contradict our other observations about humans, such as having reason, creativity, the ability to communicate, or significant relationships. This description of humans as created in the image of God would be an explanation of why these other descriptions of human beings are also true.

Some of the works of God seem to be completely continuous with what he has long been doing, whereas other works of God are new initiatives that decisively change or break previous patterns of events. God allowed the sun to rise this morning, and that was completely continuous with what he has done for many mornings in the past; the resurrection of Jesus on Easter morning was an act of God that decisively changed the previous course of what normally happens. It is worthy of notice that the account of the creation of humans in the image of God uses terminology that shows a decisive change with the previous acts of God. The rich Hebrew vocabulary has words to describe the acts of God that suggest continuity with what had previously happened, and these words are used to describe some aspects of the creation. But the writer selected words that suggest a decisive change from everything else when the creation of humans in the image of God was proclaimed. This fits with what we should all know about humans: our bodies are not so extremely different from those of many apes, and our DNA is similar to that of many animals; yet there is something decisively different about humans. While our bodies may be similar to those of a chimpanzee or a gorilla, our hearts and minds reflect the heart and mind of the Creator. And that is what is so distinctive about humans that we have a special dignity and responsibility in the universe. That God-given dignity and responsibility is the reason why humans have rights that are different from the rights of any other entity in the universe.

Careful observation of our daily experiences of ourselves and other people should give us a significant knowledge of the fact of human distinctiveness in the world. But that knowledge is easily distorted or lost. The biblical explanation that humans are created in the image of God, the ultimate Ground and Source of all beings, can deepen, protect, and clarify our knowledge of what a human being is. This is the foundation for human dignity and human rights.

3. Why Do We Need to Be Protected from Each Other?

It is inspirational to talk about human dignity; this is a topic we like. But we must never forget why this whole discussion has arisen: people regularly and repeatedly destroy other people, often using the power of the state or other powerful institutions to accomplish the greatest evils. And as part of this insidious pattern, the classic criminals against humanity often use deceptive words to explain to their followers and friends why their actions are good or necessary. The entire human rights movement is a gigantic protest against human nature as it is. The very existence of the human rights movement stands as an indictment against mankind: we are the type of beings who murder our own and occasionally even boast that in so doing we have done something good. The human rights movement shows the massive extent to which humanity is characteristically divided against itself: the light side of human nature is the bearer of the greatest dignity in creation and has been enlightened with knowledge of right and wrong; this allows humans to fight against the dark side of our nature which sometimes takes sick pleasure or finds pride in killing and destruction. Humanity is the greatest self-contradiction in the universe; but why?

Going to the early chapters of the Bible, we find the story of Cain killing Abel:

> Adam lay with his wife Eve, and she became pregnant and gave birth to Cain. She said, "With the help of the Lord I have brought forth a man." Later she gave birth to his brother Abel.
>
> Now Abel kept flocks, and Cain worked the soil. In the course of time Cain brought some of the fruits of the soil as an offering to the Lord. But Abel brought fat portions from some of the first-born of his flock. The Lord looked with favor on Abel and his offering, but on Cain and his offering he did not look with favor. So Cain was very angry, and his face was downcast.
>
> Then the Lord said to Cain, "Why are you angry? Why is your face downcast? If you do what is right, will you not be accepted? But if you do not do what is right, sin is crouching at your door; it desires to have you, but you must master it."
>
> Now Cain said to his brother Abel, "Let's go out to the field." And while they were in the field, Cain attacked his brother Abel and killed him. Genesis 4:1-8

This early account of a murder has stimulated commentators for centuries. Much of that discussion must be left for another time. It is valuable for our discussion to notice that from very early times in human history people were making a clear distinction between killing a person and killing an animal (in this case for religious worship), in spite of the obvious physical similarities between humans and animals and the similarity in the process of killing humans and animals. It is probably more valuable to notice that this early murder of a man was an expression of anger at God. Cain was angry at God because God had not accepted his sacrifice; it was very difficult for Cain to directly attack God, but it was not so difficult to attack someone who was a mirror image of God and who seemed to be a friend of God. The background of this earliest murder was *religious frustration*: hostility toward God that gets misdirected toward people. This is a key to understanding human rights problems, as well as some steps toward their management.

It is easy for the observer to notice that various types of religious frustration contribute to different types of human rights abuses. Frequently an entire people group has been persecuted because of its beliefs, whether that people group is Jewish, Christian, Hindu, Muslim, or whatever. The presence of an articulated religious system makes a people into a distinct target for people who have all sorts of hostilities and frustrations. Think of these persecuted people as being represented by Abel; their number is massive. The persecution of a religious group is rarely purely religious. Such persecutions are often mixed with ethnic hatred, economic envy, personal grudges, nationalistic zeal, and a range of other dark motives. The people committing the crimes are often broadly frustrated with life. And the well-identified religious community, religious institution, or religious leader becomes the target for violence or discrimination. Frustration with life turns into aggression toward a person or group who might be close to God. Those represented by Abel are murdered too often.

There are also those religiously frustrated people represented by Cain. Their religion or religion substitute (such as Communism, National Socialism, and various other political ideologies) makes some people or the entire movement hostile toward others and may also provide some explanation why another group of people should be hindered or destroyed. These religions or religious/political ideologies have within their doctrine and ethics certain ideas, claims, examples, or principles that explain why all other people or certain other people should be repressed, expelled, or killed. Sometimes the despised or second-class humans are identified by race, sometimes by religion, or sometimes by social class. These religions and ideologies can be grouped together as giving organized expression to internal religious frustrations, similar to those of Cain. Their religion has not provided peace with God, with themselves, or with other people. The observable results around the world are gruesome.

It is for good reason that freedom of religion is sometimes described as the "first freedom" or the "mother of human rights." The society that has learned how to protect a very extensive freedom of religion is also learning how to manage its own religious frustrations which are the root cause of many other abuses of human rights. And once those religious frustrations are largely managed, it is much easier to take steps to protect the full range of human rights. Biblical realism about human nature lets us see that protecting the freedom of religion will often also lead to the practical protection of a wide range of other human rights. Of course, real freedom of religion is both individual and collective; this means both individuals and whole communities must be allowed to give full expression to their faith.[32]

Having a deep religious need is close to the center of what makes us human; if God created us in the reflection or image of his heart and mind, it is only natural that one of our deepest drives or instincts will be for a relationship with God. When Augustine prayed, "Our hearts are restless until they find their rest in you,"

---

[32] Real freedom of religion must include such matters as freedom of speech that arise from a person's or a community's basic beliefs, e.g., freedom to educate one's children in light of one's faith, freedom to gather with fellow believers, freedom to own or rent suitable buildings or facilities for such activities. Real freedom of religion contains within it real freedom of speech, freedom of the press, freedom of assembly, freedom to travel, and freedom of education.

he was not only confessing his own desire for God.[33] He was describing a central element of what makes us human. Even though he did not believe in God, philosopher Ludwig Feuerbach claimed that what makes people human is the fact that they are religious. "Religion has its basis in the essential difference between man and the brute—the brutes have no religion." (The word "brute" meant animal.)[34] Protecting religious freedom is very close to protecting the mystery or essence of humanness.

We need to be protected from each other and from our most powerful institutions because humans have an inherited tendency to destroy each other. That tendency to destroy is closely associated with religious frustration; it often arises out of a dysfunctional religion, and/or it may be directed at people insofar as they are identified by their religious beliefs and practice. Understanding that the sources of human rights abuses are very closely connected to religious persecution gives us significant direction in knowing a first step that needs to be taken to reduce human rights abuses. That first step will often be for a society to allow people real and substantial freedom of religion.[35] And on

---

[33] This is the opening line in the famous *Confessions* of Saint Augustine (354-430), bishop of Hippo, which is in today's Algeria. This valuable book is available in various English translations and in many other languages.

[34] Ludwig Feuerbach (1804-1872) was a German atheist philosopher of religion. Some of his ideas were later adopted by Karl Marx and by Sigmund Freud, making him one of the important sources of modern European atheism. Very ironically, some of his central ideas were in his book *The Essence of Christianity*, which is an attack on Christian belief. The quotation is the opening statement of this book, which is available in various editions and languages; it is also included in many anthologies of Western philosophy.

[35] In Europe and North America, it is common to hear the claim that anyone with a clear set of beliefs will automatically want to force other people to accept those beliefs, even if violence or force is required to impose those beliefs on others. Therefore, it is claimed, skepticism or the denial of ultimate truth is needed for peace in the world. Ironically, in this manner, skeptics and nihilists attempt to coerce others to accept their belief system. As evangelicals, we insist that God is the One who convinces people of the truth of the gospel by means of his Word and Spirit, so that we renounce any use of force, violence, or coercion to convince people of the truth of the gospel. We trust in the testimony of the Holy Spirit to the truth in Christ, while we joyfully limit ourselves to using peaceful persuasion.

an individual level, we need to address our own religious frustration, our own alienation from God.

4. How Do We Know?

This important question can and should be asked about every important knowledge claim. Here we are especially asking how we know that there is a moral law distinguishing good and evil, how we know that humans are distinct from other creatures, how we know that we must be protected from each other. We cannot avoid the question of how we know these things to be true, especially when many people and cultures make contradictory claims to know many different things.

We know these matters in two ways. The two ways of knowing are alike in terms of the ultimate source of the knowledge; it comes from God. The two ways of knowing are different in terms of how that knowledge comes to us, whether through creation or through special revelation in the Bible. And the two ways of knowing are different in terms of the extent to which a person (or a culture) can reject this knowledge.

Historically, evangelical Christians have said there are two ways in which God makes himself known to the human race: special revelation, meaning God's special communication through the Bible and Christ, and creational revelation, meaning God's speech through creation.

Christian believers should acknowledge the Bible as a unique gift of God; there we find the words of eternal life, the good news about Christ. This is a revelation, a self-revealing communication, that is truly special and distinct. And while some people may be hesitant to clearly confess their highest authority, Christians should not be hesitant to confess the Bible as our highest authority.[36] In the Bible we are told about human dignity, human wickedness, and the existence of a moral law that allows us to distinguish between good and evil. These themes are not truly the center of special revelation, because the center of the Bible is the good news about Jesus; but the themes of human dignity,

---

[36] Everyone has a highest authority in his or her life, even if some people do not have the level of authenticity needed to articulate their highest authority.

human fallenness, and the moral law are essential themes that allow us to comprehend the good news about Jesus. These themes are also crucial to life in society, and many people who do not yet believe in Jesus are influenced by the biblical teaching on human nature and the moral law.

We should also acknowledge that God speaks through creation, and everything other than God is part of his creation. The apostle Paul commented on this general revelation or speech of God through creation, as well as on the ambiguous response that many people have to this type of revelation from God.

> For the wrath of God is being revealed from heaven against all the godlessness and injustice of men who suppress the truth by means of injustice, since the knowledge of God is plain in them; for God has made himself known to them. His invisible characteristics are received into consciousness through the creation of the world, namely his invisible power and divine nature, so that people are without an apology. Although they knew God, they did not glorify him or give thanks to him, but became worthless in their thoughts and their senseless hearts were darkened ... They are gossips, slanderers, God-haters, insolent, arrogant, and boastful; they invent ways of doing evil; they disobey their parents; they are senseless, disloyal, lacking in normal affections, and merciless. They know the requirement of God that those who do such things are worthy of death, but they not only do these things, they also approve those who do them. Romans 1:18-32, selections.[37]

As the apostle Paul describes the human condition, people know much more about God than they would like to know. Whether or not people want it, like it, or acknowledge it, they have a significant amount of knowledge about God and his moral law. People know at least a little about his invisible characteristics, such as mercy and justice, even if they claim to be atheists. People know at least a little about God's moral law, even if they pretend not to know there is a moral law or a God who is the Source of that moral law.

The hero of Camus's novel could pretend to try to become a "saint without God." Ironically, that attempt is possible only because all

---

[37] My own translation, as published in "Paul's Intellectual Courage in the Face of Sophisticated Unbelief," MBS Text 63, available at www.bucer.eu.

people have some God-given knowledge of right and wrong. God has written parts of his moral law into the human heart and mind, and he is continually refreshing that knowledge through his ongoing general revelation. This is what is sometimes called "the natural moral law," meaning God's moral law as it is communicated to us through nature, which is his creation. The moral law is what makes the entire human rights movement possible, for the moral law tells all people that we should do unto others as we would like them to do to us, and it also tells us that we have a duty to protect the weak and defenseless. We should see the human rights movement as a response to God's moral law revealed in his creation, even if many do not want to recognize the real source of their moral knowledge.

Genocide, the Holocaust, and numerous crimes against humanity have occurred partly because of psychopathic tyrants and inhumane ideologies. Men and women of good will should take their duties more seriously, including the duties to do unto others as we would have them do unto us and to protect the weak and defenseless. This will lead to more effective work to protect human rights. We should also acknowledge the Source of that moral demand, which is also the Source of the human dignity we should seek to protect. We also need to acknowledge that there is something like Cain in all of us, for which we need forgiveness. Genocide, the Holocaust, and crimes against humanity are only extreme forms of tendencies we all have within us, a very sobering thought.

A Challenge with Two Sides

If you call yourself a Christian, the challenge for you is to recognize that protecting the lives of people made in the image of God is a God-given responsibility. It is best if our efforts are guided by serious moral thinking informed by the Bible and the history of Christian ethics, which is one of the purposes of this little book, so we may avoid some of the well-meaning mistakes that some have made. Not all people have the same gifts and talents, so not all have to do the same thing or take up this responsibility in the same manner. Some might be called to become human rights lawyers or journalists, both of which callings will require significant training and education. But all can assist in some way, and some of these ways will be discussed in following chapters.

If you are very concerned about human rights or perhaps have even sacrificed or suffered to protect the rights of your neighbors, the challenge for you is to consider those things you know but may prefer not to know. You can attempt to become a saint without God only because of God-given knowledge about right and wrong and about the dignity of human beings created in God's image. Please consider the serious possibility that you are both responding to God's demand for justice and at the same time trying to hide from God himself. Why should you continue to hide? It seems to me that the human rights movement can be strengthened by some serious moral reflection that consciously occurs *before God*. I will try to do some of that in the following chapters.

RIGHTS, RELIGIONS, AND IDEOLOGIES

On Thursday, April 19, 2007, I opened my email, and I felt like someone had kicked me in the stomach. Terrorists had slit the throat of one of our seminary students; two of his colleagues suffered similar fates. Three men were dead, two of them Turkish, one German. Two wives were suddenly widows, and four young children had lost their fathers. They died because they were Christians; their place of death was a small Bible publishing house in Malatya, Turkey. The motives of their murderers probably arose from a mixture of nationalist ideology and the desire to enforce the demands of the Sharia, the Muslim law. Turkish nationalism says "Turkey is for Turks," with the assumption that a person who has become a Christian may no longer be a good Turk. The Muslim Sharia (at least the older interpretations of the Sharia now advocated by the new political Islam) requires the execution of men who commit treason against the community by converting from Islam to another religion, a crime of such severity that the execution may sometimes be implemented without a legal process; both Turkish victims were converts from Islam to following Jesus.[38] Perhaps their German friend just happened to be in the wrong place at the wrong time.[39]

This event made a particular truth painfully vivid to me, even though I had long understood it. Some religions, philosophies, and ideologies lead to the abuse of human rights when they are consistently implemented, whereas other religions, philosophies, and ideologies motivate people to protect human rights. Words are powerful; they shape and direct the actions of individuals,

---

[38] Some newer interpretations of the Sharia, more prominent since the 1800s, would not demand execution in these circumstances, but older interpretations of the Sharia are still influential among some people, especially in political Islam, which often follows Wahhabi theology.

[39] These murders occurred on April 17, 2007. As my personal protest against this crime, I have chosen to write these words while sitting in Turkey.

groups, and whole communities. One set of words will lead to peace, freedom, justice, and human flourishing; another set of words leads to persecution, abuse, death, and destruction. And the really important words are usually part of someone's religion, philosophy, or political ideology. Some belief systems and worldviews claim either that there is no real human dignity or that dignity is only earned by certain individuals or groups; these religions, belief systems, and worldviews can easily lead to assaults on human rights. Other belief systems and worldviews believe that dignity is given to all human beings, men, women, and children; such religions, belief systems, and ideologies tend to promote cultures, laws, and political systems that protect human rights. A serious discussion of human rights must consider the ideas which either promote or attack human rights. Too many books and articles about human rights talk as if the problems are only political or legal, neglecting the role of religions, philosophies, and ideologies in relation to human rights.

It is beyond the scope of this little book to survey all the religions, philosophies, and political ideologies of the world with regard to how they think about human dignity and human rights. What is possible is to identify selected ideas or beliefs that threaten human rights or undermine the protection of human rights, to identify some of the cultural locations where these destructive ideas occur, and to briefly state why one should reject these ideas. The critique of such destructive ideas can reduce their influence in the lives of individuals and cultures.

1. A Person Has Rights If He or She Belongs to My Race or Nation.

Because of sinful human pride, many of us would like to think that "my people," whoever they are, are somehow superior to normal mortals. Most of us quickly notice the problem when someone else regards us as inferior or subhuman because he/she belongs to a superior race. However, we might not always notice our own tendency to regard others as less than human.

While God created each of us as members of particular ethnic groups, the purpose of this identification is not to make us feel superior. On the contrary, God placed us in families and communities to give us belonging, support, and a place from which to serve other people. There is nothing wrong with a modest ethnic pride, so long as we want our neighbors of different ethnic or national groups to have a similar love of their extended family and community. I really like being a Bentheimer[40], and there is nothing wrong with those feelings as long as I truly hope that my Turkish, Czech, Russian, Vietnamese, and Roma neighbors really like belonging to their people group in the same way, and as long as the rights of the people from all the different social groups are properly protected. The serious problems start when anyone begins to imagine that his or her ethnic group or nation is significantly superior or that some other group is really inferior.[41] On some occasions, whole groups of people have talked and acted as if their race had God-like characteristics, turning their people group into an idol; for example, the Nazi glorification of "blood and race" sometimes sounded like idol worship, with their own people as the object of worship. If this line of thought is not restrained by something higher, it can lead people to think that other people groups are less than fully human. And if they are less than fully human, they do not have to be treated like fellow human beings; they do not have rights that must be protected.[42] This line of thinking has recurred repeatedly as a part of the background for ethnic cleansing and genocide.

To this point, the discussion may sound somewhat theoretical, but it is a central part of the cognitive background for some of the worst atrocities in our time. There is a clear pattern to the

---

[40] The little province of Bentheim was, for much of its history, on the border between Germany and the Netherlands.

[41] If I start telling you that we Bentheimers are a superior race, far above all the inferior peoples in the world, you will probably just laugh because you have probably never heard enough about us Bentheimers to take us seriously. If a person starts to claim superiority because he is American, Chinese, Russian, or German, you would start to recognize a moral/political problem. This is inappropriate nationalism.

[42] My wife and I have encountered the claim that it is wrong for Americans to practice prejudice against blacks, because blacks are not inherently inferior to whites; but it is proper for Europeans to practice prejudice against the Roma (also called Gypsies), because the Roma are inherently inferior to Europeans. Therefore, some claim, the Roma do not have the normal rights of humans. This line of thinking and acting should arouse our anger.

ideas which have motivated people in many bloody attempts at genocide and ethnic cleansing, in Burma, in Rwanda, in Darfur and Chad, and in the Nazi attempt to exterminate "sub-humans." Victims of genocide are routinely described as being less than fully human and therefore not in possession of the normal rights of humans; perpetrators of genocide routinely regard themselves as the true humans or as superior human beings and therefore the owners of significant rights which other people groups do not have.[43]

There may have been a time when it made sense to think that most nation-states would be comprised of people from one people group. After all, many nations had their own language, litera-ture, customs, and history which gave them their distinctive identity. In that historical situation there was a strong connec-tion between a nation and the ethnic group that led the nation. But in a global society, that is almost never true. There are now individuals from almost every language and people living in almost every nation. This makes it more important than ever to recognize that people have rights because they are human, regardless of the ethnic group to which they belong.

We can hope that most people, and especially most government authorities, will be able to recognize the common humanity of all people; this important moral truth has been recognized and

---

[43] Throughout human history, at least until the mid 1800s, there have been numerous theories that said there is no single human race. Many of these "polygenetic" theories (or myths) claimed that there are such funda-mental physical and psychological differences between the various entities sometimes called "human" that the different human "races" should be seen as entirely different creatures with different origins. Some claimed there were only four human-like races, whereas others thought there were as many as twenty-two races. Such theories were used to defend slavery of blacks in both the US and the UK in the 1800s; similar theories were used to defend the caste system in India. The ancient Greeks generally saw their "barbarian" neighbors as not human, though the Stoic philosophers disagreed with the other Greeks on this question. The fact that people from every background can have children together should be sufficient proof of the fundamental unity of the human race, which supports the idea that all people have the same natural rights. The unity of medical science and treatment is only possible because of a fundamental unity of the human race.

proclaimed by most of the important human rights documents of our time. This moral truth should be reinforced by means of Christian believers from around the world regularly and repeatedly saying that all human beings have a special dignity because they are created in the image of God. People have rights because they are human, not because of their ethnic or national identity.

2. A Person Has Rights Because He or She Belongs to My Religion.

There have been times in the history of the Christian church when some Christians did not fully recognize the political rights of people from other religions or without a well-defined religion. We must acknowledge this sin of some of our ancestors and turn away from it. This sinful idea contributed to anti-Semitism among Christians, which has recurred too often. Sinful ideas of this sort (though not using exactly this terminology) contributed to the Crusades in the eleventh through thirteenth centuries, one of the truly black times in Christian history. This problem tends to arise whenever a government becomes too closely connected with a particular religious tradition. Then that government tends to forget, neglect, or deny the rights of people who do not belong to the religious tradition most closely associated with the state. We must repeatedly and clearly say that people have rights because they are human, created in the image of God, not because they belong to my religion or our church. Within Christian circles we must say that rights come from creation, not from redemption; people have rights because they are created in the image of God, not because they believe in Jesus.

One of the examples of problems in this sphere is the relationship of Islam to the state in several countries that identify themselves as officially Muslim. In those situations, one frequently encounters the claim that a state is legitimate to the extent to which it promotes Islam. Instead of thinking of multiple religions within a state, some think of multiple states within a religion, with each state deriving its authority from that religion. It is no surprise that Jews and Christians have sometimes been assigned an official second-class status within Muslim countries, so that they have not enjoyed the privileges enjoyed by Muslims.[44] But even Jews and Christians have often been somewhat more protected than polytheists, followers of Baha'i, or people without a defined religious tradition, who have often been severely persecuted within Muslim countries. We can hope that most Muslims want to reject this pattern in the future, in the same way that Christians reject the idea of future Crusades.

It has been difficult for Muslims to successfully break with this past. Classical Muslim theology has not always had a well-developed doctrine of all humans being equally created in the image of God, though the idea of humans being in the image of God occurs occasionally in ancient Muslim texts. And recent political Islam has reasserted the claim that a Muslim state receives its legitimacy by means of promoting Islam; this means a state does not receive its moral legitimacy from protecting the rights of all people. This theological situation leaves some Muslims with an inclination to think that people have rights because they are Muslims, not because they are human. Even the more recent Muslim public human rights statements may not fully overcome this problem, because the problem has been partly rooted in traditional Muslim ways of thinking. We Christians should invite our Muslim neighbors to debate these questions with us and with each other.

A somewhat similar problem can be observed in Russian Orthodox history. The Russian Orthodox Church has a history of a close relationship with the Russian state, which is articulated in their theory of church/state relations.[45] This has been made worse by the way in which the Orthodox Church has sometimes

---

[44] This second-class legal status is usually called *dhimmitude*. It means something like restricted and protected, but the protection has usually been from extermination, not a general protection of all rights. See Bat Ye'or, *Islam and Dimmitude: Where Civilizations Collide,* translated from French by Miriam Kochman and David Littman (Associated University Presses, 2002).

[45] "Caesaropapism" is the term often used to describe a situation in which a "Caesar" or any top government ruler is accepted by the church into a "papal" or pope-like role. This tends to reduce the church to acting like a department of the government. Many Orthodox theologians insist that Caesaropapism, though often practiced by the Russian Orthodox Church, represents a distortion of proper Orthodox ethics.

become the primary institution charged with carrying and promoting Russian culture. The close relationship with the state has made it difficult for the Russian Orthodox Church to confront the Russian state when it has not protected the rights of people. At the same time, the way in which the Russian Orthodox Church has been seen as the proper carrier of the culture has left many of her own members wondering if a person who is not a member of the Russian Orthodox Church can be a good Russian. The repeated persecution of other religious groups, sometimes including evangelicals, is not surprising. Evangelical Christians need to regularly and repeatedly call on our Russian Orthodox friends to remember that all humans are created by God in the image of God; this gives people a distinctive dignity as humans, whether or not they are members of the Russian Orthodox Church. For this reason, all humans have rights which must be protected. The Orthodox Church does not need to say or do things that lead to the persecution of other religious groups in order to continue to shape Russian culture. And in an open, global society, the Orthodox Church will need to emphasize its independence from the Russian state in order to be able to articulate a proper prophetic criticism of Russian culture and society that can bring the spiritual renewal of society which our Orthodox friends desire.

3. Protecting Human Rights Leads to Radical Individualism.

It is not unusual to hear the claim that if a nation starts protecting human rights, it will almost necessarily lead to the radical, extreme individualism that is so seriously impoverishing Western society, especially Europe and North America. Some claim that other cultures, especially Asian or African cultures, have other ways of talking about political morality.

It must be granted that the most important matter is protecting real human beings, not a particular set of terms one might like to use to describe our duty to protect human life; if Asian and African cultures have other varieties of moral language to describe our duties to protect particular people, they should use that moral terminology, while carefully avoiding the tendency in all our cultural traditions to use moral language to cover up our inhumane treatment of each other. But it would be a serious mistake to accept the claim that any concern for human rights automatically commits a person to radical individualism.

I would argue that a proper concern for human rights is best maintained by an approach to life in society that avoids the extremes of individualism and collectivism. Instead of either individualism or collectivism, we should rather think that God has created multiple institutions and organisms in society, each of which has the responsibility and authority to protect, nurture, and develop human well-being in different ways. Some of these God-given institutions and organisms include family, clan, school, business, profession, medicine, church, and the different levels of government.

Some societies are more collectivist, which means they tend to think of the group, the society, the country, or the culture as being truly real and important; within the collectivist situation, the individual is important only to the extent to which he or she contributes to the larger group. The largest weakness of collectivist societies and political ideologies is that individual needs, desires, and rights are often neglected or denied. In contrast, individualist societies and ideologies say that only the individual person is real and important; the individualist may say the society or country is valuable or real only if it enables or supports the desires of individuals. The largest weakness of individualist societies and ideologies is that the individual person is worshipped as an idol, neglecting the way God gives us duties in a wide variety of relationships. Both collectivism and individualism are attempts to find safety; collectivists are usually looking for safety from the threats of nature, whereas individualists are usually looking for safety from the threats which come from the dangerous, overly powerful state. Some societies fluctuate between the two poles of collectivism and individualism.

As followers of Jesus, we should not be either collectivists or individualists. God has given us many different communities to which we can belong: family, marriage, church, neighborhood, business, school, professional organizations, cities, and nations. We can call some of these organisms and organizations "creation orders" or "creation mandates." Our task is to serve each other, really to love each other, in different ways in each of the different communities; indeed, human life flourishes when all of these different communities are fulfilling their unique God-given tasks. A central task or duty of government is to promote justice by means of protecting the rights of people. If people are serving each other in the whole range of other communities, protecting human rights does not lead to extreme individualism. Protection of human rights provides a framework of justice in society which should allow all the many other communities to pursue the duties God has assigned to each.[46]

4. Rights Are Given to People by the Government, State, or Society.

Various totalitarian and authoritarian political regimes have talked as if rights are given to people by the state, by a political party, or by the society. And it is common for such authoritarian or totalitarian regimes to be dominated by a political ideology which includes some implicit (or occasionally explicit) definition about what types of people are qualified to receive rights from the state. Within eastern European communism, economically productive members of the proletariat were supposed to be considered worthy of receiving rights from the state. Within Hitler's National Socialism, people who were carriers of true "Aryan" blood were supposed to be worthy of receiving rights, though they may not have used exactly these words to describe their point of view. Other ideologies have had other definitions about how people can earn rights from the state.

Followers of Jesus should respond to this line of thinking with several very serious criticisms. The first of these is that rights come from God, not from the state, not from the society, and not from a political party. Whenever a government, state, or political party claims to give rights to people, we should recognize idolatry; when some political entity dares to take the place of God himself, the state can easily become a devouring beast. We must

---

[46] Protestant ethics often uses the terminology of "sphere sovereignty" to describe the way in which each God-given community is directly and primarily accountable to God for fulfilling its tasks, so that each human institution or organism should also have a degree of independence in relation to other human institutions. Our Roman Catholic friends often use the terminology of "subsidiarity" to describe a similar idea, though the ideas are not 100% identical.

say at every possible occasion that rights are gifts of God, the Creator. People have rights because they are created by God in his image. But we must also recognize that many of our neighbors are not yet believers in the God of the Bible, and therefore it will be extremely difficult for them to say that rights are given by God, the Creator. This places these people in the difficult position of not knowing what to say about the origin or source of human rights.

In the European Union statements about human rights, one occasionally hears the suggestion that the EU is the source or origin of human rights, even though most of the writers probably did not really have this intention; they simply did not know what else to say about the origin of human rights. The authors of the EU statements on human rights clearly intended to say that the EU has the important task of protecting human rights; but sometimes it sounds as if it is the EU which also gives rights.

This problem has prompted people to sometimes talk about "natural rights" or to say that rights come "from nature." Many people in the past who talked about "natural rights" truly believed in God and believed that rights are gifts from God; they also knew that many of their neighbors did not believe in God; they also thought it might not be wise for the description of human rights (which the government must protect) to be too closely tied to any particular church or religion.[47] Their solution was to describe human rights as "natural" in the sense of being given by nature; sometimes they would add "and nature's God." I like it when there are public recognitions that rights come from God, but we must also recognize that the description of human rights as gifts of nature at least eliminates the horrible idolatry of saying that rights are given by the state or the government. The idolatry of the state has been a crucial part of some of the ideologies that have supported genocide; elimination of this idolatry will tend to reduce the number of genocides in the future. Without an ideology that worships the state, a class, or the party, atrocities like those under Hitler and Stalin are very hard to imagine. If a society can begin to describe human rights as

---

[47] I am thinking here especially of the descriptions of rights in philosophers such as Hugo Grotius, John Locke, and Thomas Jefferson during the time of the Enlightenment or John Finnis and Robert George in recent years.

gifts of nature, this should be recognized as an important step toward the practice of justice, which followers of Jesus must support.[48] This way of talking will reduce the idolatry of the state and the resulting abuses of people.

A second important criticism of the idea that rights are given by the state arises from the observation that what the state gives, the state can also take back again. If people get into the habit of thinking and saying that the state gives rights such as freedom of speech, freedom of religion, and freedom of assembly, then we open an important door in our minds to think or say that the state might take back what it previously gave. A major crisis or a change of regime could easily lead those in power (or a majority of the populace) to think the state may take back many important liberties that should be seen as essential parts of human dignity. Words and ideas that become accepted parts of political and legal culture have massive long-term power, for good or for evil. It should be a part of the political mission of the followers of Jesus that we attempt to convince our neighbors to talk as if rights come from nature and nature's God, not from the state. This will reduce the frequency of states taking back the rights they falsely claim to have given to their people; and this will reduce the number of abuses of those rights.

A third important criticism of the idea that a state can give rights arises from seeing the way in which states tend to think they may give rights to some people and withhold rights from other people. Christians should be familiar with the time the apostle Paul claimed his rights as a Roman citizen (see Acts

---

[48] Many of the writers of the seventeenth and eighteenth centuries who talked about "natural rights" were Deists, if they were not Christians. As Deists they believed in a Designer who created the world but did not continue to be active in the world in the works of providence, redemption, and revelation. Today the description of human rights as gifts of nature raises the danger of encouraging "Mother Nature" or "Mother Earth" worship, which is usually more pantheistic, without clear distinctions between a creator, nature, and human beings. "Mother Nature" worship can sometimes confuse the distinction of humans from non-humans, so that people do not have a clear explanation of why humans have rights which are not shared by insects or oysters. We must never grow tired of repeating that humans are distinct because we are created in the image of God.

22:22-29). By Roman laws of the time, many people could be flogged, whipped, or otherwise tortured in order to gain a confession of guilt regarding a crime; Roman citizens had a legal right not to be tortured and not to be punished without a trial. Paul claimed his rights as a citizen, and the soldiers were horrified that they had nearly committed the serious crime of torturing a citizen. Torturing non-citizens was business as usual, since the ideology of the Roman Empire regarded rights as something that could be given by the empire to selected people, particularly its own citizens, who were very few in number.

This same problem has occurred repeatedly around the world. When people think the government is the source or giver of rights, they will tend to withhold those rights from anyone who is seen as less desirable, and those less desirable people may be tortured, punished, or killed without question. Christians and all people of good will must shout with one voice that people have rights because they are human, not because of any particular citizenship or any legal situation, class level, or political status. The state does not give rights, and it may not decide who has rights. The state must observe and protect human rights, even of the people it regards as its enemies.

5. People Are Given Rights by International Law, Treaties, and Human Rights Conventions.

Over the last several decades, starting mostly after World War II, we have seen a developing body of international laws, treaties, and human rights conventions, some of which have been implemented and followed by various national or international courts. Most of this has been very good; some people are being called to account for genocide, war crimes, and some other crimes against humanity. Otherwise these criminals would not have faced justice in this life. Many judges and lawyers have made great personal sacrifices to establish these systems of international justice. Their efforts are reducing the number of times that terrible atrocities go unpunished because the criminals had manipulated local laws or legal systems prior to committing their worst crimes.

At the same time, this very constructive development may ironically share in the very problem it is intended to overcome: the idea that an action is acceptable if there is not a specific law forbidding the action. A good example of the problem is the profoundly disturbing dilemma faced by the judges at both the European and Asian war crimes trials after World War II. Many of the atrocities committed by Japanese and Nazi leaders during the war, as well as during the general social chaos surrounding the war, were not illegal under the laws of their countries. Some national laws were changed or abolished prior to the crimes, so the horrible actions were not illegal. Should the judges have declared these people "not guilty" because they had not broken any written laws, even though the judges knew without doubt that many of the accused had caused the deaths of millions, in addition to causing unspeakable suffering? Can an action be illegal, even if there is no law specifically forbidding the action? Some of the judges concluded that there must be a law above the law, a universal moral law above the written civil law, and that this unwritten law is clear enough to provide a basis for a trial at law in extraordinary circumstances.[49]

The good efforts since that time have reduced the problem by means of putting into place a network of international laws, tribunals, and human rights treaties that should clearly document what a crime against humanity is. The size of the intellectual dilemma faced by the World War II war crimes tribunals has been minimized; in our time the justices serving in trials of criminals against humanity have much more support and guidance by means of written laws and treaties. But the basic problem has not disappeared.

Some people describe this problem as "Legal Positivism." Legal Positivism is any theory that says either that there is no law above the law or that we cannot know if there is a law above the law. It is not surprising that the horrible totalitarian regimes of the twentieth century advocated positivist legal theories, claiming there is no higher law by which the actions of their party or state could be evaluated. What is deeply disturbing is the extent

---

[49] A concise analysis of this question appears in *Ethics: Theory and Practice,* edited by Manual Velasquez and Cynthia Rostankowski (Prentice Hall, 1985), pp. 31-34.

to which some of the legal theories in democracies are also posi-tivistic.[50]

Within a democratic context, the idea is often encountered that a law or policy is just and proper if it came into existence by means of a proper democratic process, whether by means of a popular vote or coming from a congress or parliament. Such theories ignore the possibility that some actions, laws, or policies may be unjust by nature, meaning that the actions, law, or policies can never be practiced in a just manner. Such theories ignore the possibility that justice is something real, prior to a particular law we vote into existence. It is possible, for example, that a democ-racy will adopt and enforce laws that are cruel and unjust in their treatment of minorities or in their treatment of people who are not citizens. A positivist theory of law and human rights makes it very difficult for anyone to say a law or policy is funda-mentally wrong. And some actions are unjust, even if they are allowed by democratically adopted laws.

We must avoid ever talking about human rights in a merely positivistic manner. I have repeatedly heard this problem among my university students. Without deeply considering the question, they have talked as if people have those rights, and only those rights, which have been assigned or recognized by international law or international human rights treaties. This is an exact reversal of how we should talk. People have rights because of a God-given dignity, which is part of the image of God in humans. International law and human rights treaties should serve to protect and honor these rights, not give those rights. If we say that rights are given by international law or by treaties, someone else will want to change those laws or treaties (or important definitions of terms) and take those rights away again. This problem is very similar to the problem of saying that rights are given by a government or by society. Such a positivistic interpre-tation of human rights laws and declarations will undermine the

---

[50] See Phillip E. Johnson, "The Modernist Impasse in Law," in *God & Culture: Essays in Honor of Carl F. H. Henry,* edited by D. A. Carson and John D. Woodbridge (Grand Rapids: Eerdmans, 1993), pp. 180-194; David Noble, *Understanding the Times* (Summit Press, 1991), pp. 499-593; and Emil Brunner, *Christianity and Civilisation, Part II* (New York: Scribner's Sons, 1949), pp. 101-113.

effectiveness of the people who invested so much time, effort, and love in the creation of just laws and declarations.

To reduce this problem, we should clearly distinguish between civil rights and natural (God-given) human rights. People have civil rights because of membership or participation in particular societies; people have natural human rights because they are human. I happen to be a citizen of one country but a long-term resident of another country; this means I have slightly different civil rights in the two countries. I can vote in one country, where I am a citizen; I might receive social security benefits in a country in which I am not a citizen. My civil rights are determined by the laws of the two countries in which I have a legal status (as well as by a vast range of international agreements). But I also have certain moral rights that belong to me because I am a human being, without regard to citizenship or residency in any country. As a human being, I have rights to life, to speak my mind, to worship, to own property, to freedom from torture, to freedom of travel, etc. These fundamental human rights are real and important, whether or not they are recognized by international law, treaties, or human rights declarations. The valuable international measures are properly intended to confirm, clarify, and protect human rights; they do not create or give those rights.

6. Human Rights Come from the Self.

This point of view is not usually stated in exactly these words; therefore, even students of philosophy sometimes miss the central claims. Points of view like this are often encountered in individualistic, secular, Western liberalism, which has been very influential in North American universities and in the media. Michael Tooley is a representative philosopher of this perspective; he was largely following the theories of Joel Feinberg, who claimed that the type of entity or being that can have rights is the type of entity or being that can have interests. Tooley argues, "The interest principle tells us that an entity cannot have any rights at all, and a fortiori, cannot have a right to life, unless it is capable of having interests." From this basis he continues his argument by claiming that in order to have interests, one must have consciousness and an awareness of the self as a subject of continuing consciousness. I cried the first time I read the conclusion to this argument. "It is seen to be most unlikely that human fetuses, or even newborn babies, possess any concept of a continuing self ... This means that such individuals do not possess a right to life." He continues, "... It becomes very much an open question whether animals belonging to other species do not possess properties that give them a right to life. Indeed, I am strongly inclined to think that adult members of at least some nonhuman species do have a right to life."[51]

The background for Tooley's worldview is naturalistic (meaning atheistic) evolution which regards life as a result of chance. If life is a result of chance, then human life is also a result of chance. This leaves no clear and clean distinction between human life and nonhuman life, so that humanity is not seen as qualitatively different from that which is not human. From this starting point, he writes about rights. The basic framework of his theory of ethics is that consciousness leads to interests; interests lead to moral rights; moral rights should be systematically recognized and protected by law in a rational manner.

We should be deeply disturbed by Tooley's defense of abortion and the killing of babies; very arbitrarily he thinks developed societies should not allow infanticide on children over an age of about a week. Prior to that time they are disposable. He really claims that some animals have more rights than human babies. This perspective arises from his broader picture of the source of any type of moral rights which should also be recognized by law. Rights come to the self *from the self.* Though the ideas are not usually so clearly articulated, something similar is common in Western individualism. Many assume, perhaps vaguely, that rights are given to the self by the self, which some animals can also do.

Theories of this type, especially when not clearly articulated, have two negative influences on human rights protection. Someone will write a human rights statement that sounds like a small child writing a list of all the gifts he or she wants for Christmas;

---

[51] Michael Tooley, "In Defense of Abortion and Infanticide," in *Applying Ethics: A Text with Readings,* fourth edition, edited by Jeffrey Olen and Vincent Barry (Wadsworth, 1992), pp. 176-185. Quotations from pages 178, 183, and 185.

anything and everything that might serve someone's self-interest becomes a "right" which people should have. In this way, the serious discussion of human rights is reduced to nonsense which no one should take seriously; this is one of the reasons why some morally sensitive people want to drop any discussion of human rights. If we say rights come from nature, at least we can have a sober discussion of what rights people may have. Additionally, Tooley's type of argument both reflects and promotes the loss of any morally significant difference between humans and non-human animals. We should not be cruel to animals, but the protection of human rights will be dependent on keeping a clear distinction in our minds between the value of humans and that of animals.

7. We Earn Rights by Means of Abilities and Functions.

Another important claim we encounter in individualistic secular liberalism is that human rights are closely tied to normal human abilities and functions. The widely read animal rights philosopher Peter Singer has argued that a right to life is properly based on such normal human abilities as self-awareness, being able to plan for the future, and being able to carry on meaningful relationships. These abilities, he claims, are what give normal humans rights which mice do not have. However, he claims, a well-developed dog, pig, or chimpanzee may possess these abilities to a larger degree than does a severely retarded child or an adult with severe senility. Therefore, he thinks some animals have rights that some humans do not have.[52]

I often thought about Singer's theories during the several years when my mother-in-law was disabled with Alzheimer's disease. My wife's mother, once a very intelligent and active woman, lost most of the normal abilities and functions which, Singer claimed, give us human rights. She could not plan for the future or carry on meaningful relationships; I do not know about the level of her self-awareness during her final years. According to Singer, our family dog had more rights than she did; and if I did not agree with Singer, he claimed I would be guilty of the serious sin of "speciesism." He carefully chose his moral language so this sin

---

[52] See Peter Singer, *Animal Liberation* (New York, 1975).

would sound like racism and sexism, the unjust treatment of a person because of the person's race or gender.

Theories of human value like that of Singer can be called "functionalist" in the sense that human dignity is based on normal human functions and abilities. And most functionalist theories of human dignity, whether argued by Western secular philosophers or by communism theorists, lead to the conclusion that people who do not have those functions do not have any rights. Those people may be discarded, whether via active euthanasia, infanticide, or a concentration camp.

In stark contrast, I understand the biblical claim to be that human dignity comes to us as a gift from God. For that reason, I would prefer to call it an "alien dignity," meaning a dignity that comes to us from outside ourselves as a gift. This terminology is derived from the way evangelicals have often called our righteousness in Christ an "alien righteousness," meaning a righteousness that comes to us as a gift from God while we are still sinners.[53] It is not a righteousness that comes from within us; our righteousness in Christ comes as a free gift from God. In a similar manner, our dignity as humans is not really something inherent or intrinsic. It is extrinsic or exherent, coming to us from outside, from God, because he has called us to be in his image. Human dignity exists because that is how God has decided to view us. A dignity of this type cannot be lost because Alzheimer's disease or any other disability destroys our normal human functions. And therefore we should say that people have rights that are not based on normal functions and abilities. Human dignity is a free gift of God to all men, women, and children.

---

[53] This way of talking about an "alien" righteousness in Christ was used already by Martin Luther in the early sixteenth century; he may have learned it from someone earlier. The term "alien dignity" was probably coined by the German Protestant ethicist Helmut Thielicke in the mid-twentieth century to show the difference between biblically informed theories of human dignity and those theories which are influenced by unbelief.

Comments

Human rights abuses are often called "crimes against humanity." The value of this way of talking is that it calls these actions crimes and thereby makes it clear that people can and should be held accountable before a judge in a court of law for their actions. This is a very large advantage. The disadvantage of this way of talking is that it can accidentally hide the way in which human rights abuses are often significantly different from other crimes. Human rights abuses are often closely tied to a political ideology, a dysfunctional religion, or a set of philosophical convictions which are used to justify criminal behavior. The enforcement of international laws against human rights abuses must be accompanied by the critique of the ideas that lead to such human rights abuses and a bold proclamation that God created people with special dignity in his image.

Some evangelical Christians will be called by God to become specialists in human rights law, human rights journalism, or other forms of specialized activism. I have been inspired by the example of William Wilberforce, who spent much of his career tirelessly fighting in the British Parliament for laws against slave trading. In addition to these specialists, many evangelical Christians can also become critics of the ideas which support human rights abuses. God calls us to speak out against sin on the basis of his Word. This is part of Christian proclamation which should be central to many of our meetings as Christians. The condemnation of sin must also include a condemnation of the ideas that support such sinful behavior, whether the sins are committed by individuals, political parties, or governments. We should publicly criticize the ideas and beliefs that support human rights abuses in our sermons, Bible classes, youth groups, schools, colleges, and seminaries. There are, today, hundreds of millions of evangelical Christians scattered around the globe. We must have millions of churches, Bible study groups, prayer groups, and Sunday School classes. If we start criticizing the ideas and beliefs that lead to human rights abuses, we can slowly have a global impact that parallels the efforts of human rights declarations and courts. This is, I think, part of what it means to love our neighbors in a global society.

We must always be careful not to let a Christian church or an evangelical mission become a political party. But we should publicly criticize the ideas and beliefs that attack the only proper image of God within creation, human beings, expecting that this criticism will have an influence in the public square. The Bible gives us the most exalted view of human nature available today, when many people do not know what to say about what a human being is or why human life has any dignity. We should publicly proclaim what the Bible says about the value of human life, expecting this proclamation to contribute to cultures and policies. We should let the world know that we think that humans have a God-given dignity; we can do this by talking about it frequently. This may help people of good will come to faith, push various political leaders and their parties in a positive direction on these questions, cause changes in political ideologies, and even influence our neighbors who follow some other religion. The voices of hundreds of millions of evangelical Christians can influence public opinion around the world. To help protect human rights, we should tell the world that human life has a special God-given value.

HUMAN DIGNITY AND RIGHTS: MY CHRISTIAN PERSPECTIVE

October 10, 1856. Hudson Taylor was traveling on a river boat to Ningpo, China.

Among his fellow passengers, one Chinese, who had spent some years in England and went by the name of Peter, was much upon his heart, for, though not unacquainted with the Gospel, he knew nothing of its saving power. Simply he told the story of this man's friendliness and his own efforts to win him to Christ. Nearing the city of Sung-kiang, they were preparing to go ashore together to preach and distribute tracts, when Mr. Taylor in his cabin was startled by a splash and cry that told of a man overboard. Springing at once on deck, he looked round and missed Peter.

"Yes," exclaimed the boatman unconcernedly, "it was over there he went down!"

To drop the sail and jump into the water was the work of a moment; but the tide was running out, and the low, shrubless shore afforded little landmark. Searching everywhere in an agony of suspense, Mr. Taylor caught sight of some fishermen with a dragnet, just the thing needed.

"Come," he cried, as hope revived, "come and drag over this spot. A man is drowning!"

"*Veh bin*," was the amazing reply: "It is not convenient."

"Don't talk of convenience! Quickly come, or it will be too late."

"We are busy fishing."

"Never mind your fishing! Come—only come *at once*! I will pay you well."

"How much will you give us?"

"Five dollars! (worth at the time more than 30 shillings) only don't stand talking. Save life without delay!"

"Too little!" they shouted across the water." We will not come for less than thirty dollars."

"But I have not so much with me! I will give you all I've got."

"And how much may that be?"

"Oh, I don't know. About fourteen dollars."

Upon this they came, and the first time they passed the net through the waters brought up the missing man. But all Mr. Taylor's efforts to restore respiration were in vain. It was only too plain that life had fled, sacrificed to the callous indifference of those who might easily have saved it.[54]

The fishermen in this story were probably no worse than many millions of other people around the world, but the contrasting priorities and actions of Hudson Taylor and of the men in the boat vividly portray contrasting worldviews, especially contrasting views of the value of human life. Taylor, as a follower of Jesus, saw the drowning man as having an eternal destiny and therefore as bearing immeasurable dignity and unspeakable value. The man in the water was created in the image of God. Without a second thought, Taylor would stop the boat, jump into the river, and spend his last dollar to save him; the men in the boat had to be extremely well paid to spend a little time to try to save a drowning man. Otherwise, human life was not worth saving or protecting; callous indifference to needless, preventable suffering and death comes all too easily unless people and cultures are taught that human life has a special value.

It is a part of the human predicament that we forget our own dignity, as well as the dignity of our neighbors; we forget that we are created in the image of God, the Creator of the entire universe. Instead of recognizing the dignity God has given to us and to our neighbors, we usually substitute pride, the vain attempt to imagine that we are better than someone else. We imagine that we (individually or as a group) are smarter, faster, richer, or better looking than anyone else, even if we are too polite (more polite than anyone else!) to say it very often. Such pride is not only silly and sinful; it is also a witness to something far greater. Pride is possible only because of a partly forgotten dignity that has been turned upside-down and then inflated like a balloon.

---

[54] Dr. and Mrs. Howard Taylor, *Hudson Taylor and the China Inland Mission: The Growth of a Work of God* (London: Morgan & Scott, 1920), pp. 4-6. The language used here is probably influenced by free translation from Chinese into mid-nineteenth-century English.

Pride is possible only because of how God has made us; neither my dog nor my computer is proud. Recognizing and understanding our God-given dignity is a step toward overcoming pride and promoting a more humane and God-honoring way of life, individually, in our churches, and in society. The recognition of human dignity is a key step toward recovering from silly personal pride.

1. The Theological Foundations of Human Dignity

Psalm 8 is not well enough known among Christians or in society more broadly:

> O Lord, our Lord,
> how majestic is your name in all the earth!
>
> You have set your glory above the heavens.
>
> From the lips of children and infants you have ordained praise because of your enemies, to silence the foe and the avenger.
>
> When I consider your heavens, the work of your fingers,
> the moon and stars which you have set in place,
> what is man that you are mindful of him,
> the son of man that you care for him?
>
> You made him a little lower than the heavenly beings
> and crowned him with glory and honor.
>
> You made him ruler over the works of your hands;
> you put everything under his feet:
> all flocks and herds, and the beasts of the field,
> the birds of the air and the fish of the sea,
> all that swim the paths of the seas.
>
> O Lord, our Lord,
> how majestic is your name in all the earth!

The psalm writer is clearly thinking about the creation and commissioning of men and women as described in the first chapters of Genesis. He is overwhelmed by the majesty of creation; and when he thinks about human beings and the role God has given us in creation, he is even further overwhelmed. What is a human being? Created by God to be a little lower than the heavenly beings, crowned by God with glory and honor, and commissioned by God to be his deputy ruler or caretaker over all of the rest of creation. Very clearly the Psalmist sees humans as having a very distinct role in the entire universe: something like the rest of creation because we are created; something like God because of the unique dignity, commission, and task given by God.[55] And to what the psalmist writes we could add: God set eternity in our hearts; God has given us desires for justice, mercy, and faithfulness that are the image of his justice, mercy, and faithfulness; God has given us senses and a mind that can partly (but really) understand his creation and God himself. God has given us such a remarkable dignity and worth; how could Hudson Taylor *not* stop the boat, jump into the water, and try to save a creature of such dignity, a human being! But like the men in the fishing boats, individuals and whole cultures forget our God-given dignity.

This incredible human dignity was confirmed by the Incarnation: God became a human being, a Jewish man, in the person of Jesus Christ. In the early days of the Christian church, many people struggled to comprehend the proclamation that Jesus was both fully God and fully human. This central Christian claim was almost too much for the human mind to accept; probably for this reason some doubted his humanity while others doubted his full deity. Because human reason is darkened and weakened by sin, even Christian believers found it easier to think that Jesus Christ was either a very special man (but not fully God) or a manifestation of God (but not fully human.) And yet the witness of the Scriptures is that Jesus is both fully God and fully human. As the apostle John writes about Jesus, "In the beginning was the Word, and the Word was with God, and the Word was God. He was with God in the beginning. Through him all things were made; without him nothing was made that has been made." And then a few lines later he adds, "The Word became flesh and made his dwelling among us." (John 1:1-3; 14)

What we must not miss is the claim about human beings: nothing else in all of creation has the unique privilege of God having

---

[55] It is important that we keep a clear line in our minds between the Creator and the creation; this will help keep us from falling into pantheism, which does not keep a clear line between an infinite, personal Creator and his creation. It is also important to keep a clear line in our minds between humans and the rest of creation; only human beings are in the image of God.

taken on its nature. God became a human. Only humans have this distinctive rank and dignity. God created mountains and seas, stars and planets, along with plants and animals of all varieties. Each has its distinct place and value within his creation, but God did not take on the nature of any of these. God became a real human being; he was born as a baby and grew up into full human maturity. The Incarnation corresponds with the previous work of God, that of creating humans in his own image. And the account of the Incarnation provides a confirmation of human dignity and value which is distinctive to the Christian faith.

Our appreciation of human dignity should be further strengthened by God's work of salvation. As an evangelical Christian, I am very comfortable quoting John 3:16: "For God so loved the world that he gave his one and only son, that whoever believes in him should not perish but have eternal life." These wonderful words quickly turn our minds to our eternal hope. Our first response should be one of gratitude and a life filled with hope. But as a second or third response to these words, we should notice the distinctive dignity of humans: God established a costly plan to save humans, a plan that cost the life and suffering of Jesus. And though the plan of salvation seems to include some benefits for all of creation, salvation is especially intended for human beings. People, and nothing else in creation, can respond to the gospel with faith, hope, and love. The distinctive role of humans as conscious recipients of God's salvation further confirms the unique dignity of human beings. Of course there are many people who have not yet believed in the salvation offered by faith in Christ, but we should regard all people as potential believers. The gospel of Christ should confirm and strengthen our appreciation of the dignity of all humans in the sight of God.

Sin makes people forget their own God-given dignity, as well as the value of the lives of their neighbors. The biblical message brings us not only the great treasure of the gospel of God's grace; it also brings us a powerful reminder of who we are as humans. Our dignity as created in the image of God is confirmed and explained by the special commission as God's deputies who must care for his world, as well as by the Incarnation and the work of salvation. This should give Christians a profound, deep, and enduring grasp of the value of the lives of humans which should be attractive to the many people who do not have an explanation of who we are. These truths about ourselves should not only shape our own lives and transform the organizations led by Christians. These truths can also flow out from the Body of Christ into our various cultures to make them more humane.

There was a stark contrast between the Chinese boat people Hudson Taylor knew in 1856 and the government of the Republic of China after the earthquakes in early 2008. Even though there were probably some mistakes and failures, the Chinese government made a serious effort to protect and save its people after this devastating earthquake. And even though the reasons for this proper course of action may never be fully articulated and explained, the actions themselves bear witness to a perception or intuition of the value of human life. This is a substantial change from the feelings of the boatmen in 1856. Why? There are probably several parts to the answer. At least one part of the answer is that during the last 150 years, many Christians have forcefully reminded our neighbors of the value of human life. This has been done by word and by deed. Whether Christians have been preaching a biblical message about the creation and salvation of human beings, or establishing programs and organizations (e.g., orphanages, hospitals, schools, humanitarian aid organizations) that take care of those people, Christians have been powerfully reminding our neighbors that we (and our God) are convinced that human life has a special value. And that message can begin to influence our neighbors, even if they do not fully accept the biblical message. We should be very happy when that happens. And now we need to speak even more clearly and powerfully about human rights.

2. Rights and Christian Wisdom

Talking about human rights and defending human rights should arise from a perception of the value and dignity of human life. It is unfortunate that many times when people mention "rights," it sounds like something trivial and even selfish. Someone says, "I have my rights," while someone else says, "You have no right to do that." Serious moral discussion has degenerated into silly assertions of what people like or dislike. Such silly claims made about such an important topic have encouraged some skeptical philosophers to suggest that all moral claims (and especially those made about "rights") are nothing more than statements of what we like or dislike, mere emotional preferences, not too different from our preferences about types of food or clothes.[56] We must strongly disagree with this skepticism, but we must also say that there are many mistakes when people talk about supposed rights. I think many of the mistakes that some make while talking about human rights can be reduced by the light of the biblical worldview.

I have already argued that we should not confuse justice with mercy. It was the demand of justice that required the full payment for the guilt of our sins, a payment which was made by Jesus on the cross. It was mercy that moved God to make that payment in the Person of Jesus. Justice and mercy can fit together and work together because both mercy and justice correlate with the value of the people who need both mercy and justice. But mercy and justice should not be confused with each other. "Human rights" is the moral language of justice. To say that someone's rights are not properly protected means that justice has not been done. This is often different from saying a person or group of people needs mercy. And the needs for mercy and for justice are very different from the selfish desires and preferences that often lead people to say "I have my rights" or "You have no right."

Because of the silly selfishness we hear so often when people say "I have my rights," some morally sensitive Christians have wondered if it is really proper for Christians to claim their moral and legal rights. Part of the proper Christian life is learning to turn away from selfishness. But then we read about the apostle Paul claiming his legal rights from the Roman government (Acts 22:23-30), and some do not know what to think. The solution, I think, is to see that there are times when it is proper to claim our rights, but not all claims to rights are true claims. Paul was simply demanding that the government of his time practice

---

[56] Philosophers often use the term "emotivism" to describe the theory that all moral claims are only the expression of emotions. Christians should reject emotivist moral theories because we believe there is a real right and wrong.

justice, the exact thing which governments are especially supposed to do. This was not in any way selfish. We, too, can use the language of human rights to demand that governments practice justice, including how they treat us and our families; it is false and morally silly to use the language of human rights to demand that other people give us anything we might happen to desire.

One of the earlier Christian ethicists to write on the topic of human rights was Thomas Aquinas (1225-1274). Though what he wrote on the topic was brief, his incisive analysis is very constructive. St. Thomas asks, "Are we morally obligated to obey human laws?" His question assumes his distinctions between the four types of laws: (1) the eternal law, which exists in the reason or mind of God; (2) the natural law, which is the reflection or image of the eternal law written by creation into human reason; (3) the divine law, which is the special revelation of God in the Bible; and (4) human law, the very fallible rules written and enforced in every society.[57] The answer St. Thomas gives to his own question is very interesting.

> The ordinances human beings enact may be just or unjust. If they are just, then we have a moral obligation to obey them, since they ultimately derive from the eternal law of God ... An ordinance may be unjust for one of two reasons: first, it may be contrary to the rights of humanity; and second, it may be contrary to the rights of God.[58]

---

[57] For more on how the theology and philosophy of law synthesized by St. Thomas can be appropriated within Protestant ethics, see Thomas K. Johnson, *Natural Law Ethics: An Evangelical Proposal* (Bonn: Verlag für Kultur und Wissenschaft, 2005).

[58] Thomas Aquinas, *Summa Theologica,* question 96, article 4. The translation used here is that of Manuel Velasquez (Copyright 1983), an excerpt of which appears in *Ethics: Theory and Practice,* edited by Manuel Velasquez and Cynthia Rostankowski (Prentice Hall, 1985), pp. 41-54. The quotation is from pages 52 and 53. There are some significant Latin-to-English translation questions in this text. Some translations use the term "human good" instead of "rights of humanity;" I think the term "rights of humanity" fits the context better than does "human good." The choice Thomas made to locate his discussion of human rights within his discussion of the natural moral law indicates that he saw human rights as an organic part of the natural moral law. Aquinas saw the natural law as God's moral (and physical/scientific) law which is built into creation and into properly

The conclusions that Thomas draws from this assessment is that people have no strict moral obligation to obey unjust laws, though prudence requires great caution before deciding to disobey a law. However, in some situations, one may have a moral obligation to disobey an unjust law, which is to practice civil disobedience. According to Thomas Aquinas, the essential function of human rights claims is to show that a governmental action, policy, or law is so seriously unjust that morally sensitive Christians should consider disobeying the government. One must sometimes consider disobeying human laws because they are frequently unjust; but when a human law is just, then all people have a God-given moral obligation to obey the human laws.

3. But What Rights?[59]

From the time of Aquinas until today, there have been many changes in the way people talk about the societal functions of human rights claims and in the claims about what rights people have. It is my assessment that not all of these changes in the way people talk about human rights have been good changes. Some statements in the important public human rights declarations seem to be informed by ideologies which we Christians should reject, even though we will want to affirm most of the content of most of the important human rights declarations.

In the early twenty-first century, it is common for people to talk about three "generations" of human rights.[60] First-generation rights are primarily about what a government, person, or organization should *not* do to people. Read, for example, Articles 3

---

functioning practical reason. Because the natural moral law comes from God through creation, the content is the same as the moral law specially revealed in the Bible. Even people without the Bible receive some benefit from the natural moral law.

[59] I learned much of what is in this section from Dr. Paul Marshall in lectures he gave at the European Humanities University, Minsk, Belarus, in 1994. His contribution to an evangelical view of human rights theory is summarized in his essay "Human Rights" in *Toward an Evangelical Public Policy*, edited by Ronald J. Sider and Diane Knippers (Grand Rapids: Baker, 2005), pp. 307-322.

[60] This way of classifying different types of rights was probably started by the Czech political theorist Karel Vasak in the 1970s.

through 23 of the United Nations Universal Declaration of Human Rights, which appears at the end of this chapter.

This is a very good statement of what are now called "first generation" human rights. Some of the people who helped to write these words were very thoughtful Christians, and some of the others were influenced by the biblical vision of the value of human life.[61] A few of these rights can be twisted under the influence of mistaken ideologies, such as when the right to privacy (Article 12) is used as a legal defense of abortion in the United States today. But when carefully interpreted, Christians should fully endorse and advocate these rights as corresponding with our understanding of the God-given dignity of human beings. A world that observed and protected these rights would enjoy much more justice, as well as the peace that often results from justice. I think that the clear, public articulation of these rights is a gift of God's common grace.[62]

The so-called second-generation rights are very different. A classical statement of second-generation rights is found in Articles 24 and 25 of the United Nations Universal Declaration of Human Rights, which is to be found at the end of this chapter.

Here we have moved from fundamental freedoms and protections to a very different type of claim, that the State has a strong duty to provide certain services to all its residents. I do not think this is a wise use of moral language, since it is a confusion of the moral demand that we practice justice (which includes protecting rights) with the moral demand that we practice mercy and loyalty. We should be very concerned about matters such as food, clothing, housing, and medical care for people in need, but this should be described as mercy (or in some situations, as acts of loyalty), not primarily as the practice of justice. This confusion may have the unintended consequence that it weakens the public concern for basic, first-generation human rights. Statements like

---

[61] One of the very thoughtful Christians I have in mind here is Dr. Charles Malik, the deep, God-fearing philosopher and diplomat from Lebanon. He influenced all the other people who participated in writing the UN Human Rights Declaration.

[62] "Common grace" is a way of describing those gifts of God which make human life possible and possibly humane. "Special grace" is a way of describing salvation in Christ.

Article 25 may easily discredit some claims to violations of human rights, for suddenly it sounds like there is a moral equivalency between a government not providing very high unemployment benefits and a government selling people (or allowing people to be sold) into slavery. Even worse, a comparison of Article 24 with Article 9 could make a naïve reader think that arbitrarily sending a person into exile or prison is no worse than if the government does not provide adequate paid holidays. Articles 24 and 25 sound like a wish list for all the characteristics of a humane society; they also sound as if we can have as many rights as we want, because rights come from the self. It bears repeating that such arbitrary claims to unlimited lists of rights can easily discredit the entire effort to seriously protect human rights in the name of justice.

It was probably in reaction to this article of the UN human rights declaration (and similar statements in other human rights declarations) that the writers of the important Oxford Declaration on Christian Faith and Economics (1990) commented (paragraph 49):

> With the United Nations Declaration of Human Rights, the language of human rights has become pervasive throughout the world. It expresses the urgent plight of suffering people whose humanity is daily being denied them by their oppressors. In some cases rights language has been misused by those who claim that anything they want is theirs "by right." This breadth of application has led some to reject rights as a concept, stating that if everything becomes a right then nothing will be a right, since all rights imply corresponding responsibilities. Therefore it is important to have clear criteria for what defines rights.[63]

"If everything becomes a right, then nothing will be a right." This is the center of the problem with the second generation of human rights. It is a significant problem that has cheapened the entire discussion of human rights around the world. At this point in the history of human rights discussion, it is almost impossible to

---

[63] "The Oxford Declaration on Christian Faith and Economics," in *On Moral Business: Classical and Contemporary Resources for Ethics in Economic Life,* edited by Max L. Stackhouse, Dennis P. McCann, and Shirley J. Roels with Preston Williams (Grand Rapids: Eerdmans, 1995), pp 479-480.

remove the second generation of rights from the now standard lists of human rights (such as the UN Declaration). And Christians should be grateful that many of our neighbors who do not yet believe in Christ are sensitive to the moral principles of mercy and loyalty, even if they lack the light of the cross which allows Christian believers to clearly distinguish the moral demands of mercy from the moral demands of justice. But the inclusion of second-generation economic rights in the standard lists of human rights makes all human rights sound like distant, vague political goals to be pursued at some later date in human history, not as demands of justice which can and should be met *today*, demands which can usually be met by someone (often a representative of a government or a military force) refraining from doing something which is unjust.

An excellent analysis of this problem comes from Paul Marshall:

> The problem with treating economic provisions as if they were rights is that there are often legitimate reasons why a particular government would not be able to fulfill such rights at a given historical juncture. Even a well-meaning government may not be able to guarantee income, or housing, or health care, or even food. Many African countries simply do not have the resources to do so. Consequently, if we were to treat economic guarantees as rights, then we would be forced to accept that rights cannot and need not be met immediately. They would be things *aimed for* rather than *guaranteed*. The result is that we will end up diluting rights to mere goals and denying their immediacy.[64]

I would strongly emphasize that the reason I think it was not wise to include such normal human *needs* as housing, health care, income, food, or social services in lists of *rights* is precisely because I so strongly want to see the real needs of people met. Across the last half of the twentieth century, in those countries where first-generation human rights were generally well-protected, natural sympathy for the needs of others moved people to also take effective steps to care for people in need. Justice

---

[64] Paul Marshall, "Human Rights," in *Toward an Evangelical Public Policy,* edited by Ronald J. Sider and Diane Knippers (Grand Rapids: Baker, 2005), p. 320.

provides a social context within which mercy flourishes.[65] Additionally, in those countries where there is real freedom of speech, freedom of the press, and freedom of religion, the publicity given to significant suffering will give rise to humanitarian aid efforts that take care of those in the greatest need.[66] Stated in other terms, many of the world's greatest needs for food, housing, clothing, and medical care occur in those countries with the world's worst records with regard to first-generation human rights: North Korea, Myanmar, and Sudan. The lack of foundational justice contributes to grinding, destructive poverty and even starvation.

In light of the way the Bible distinguishes between justice and mercy, and in light of the way Thomas Aquinas and other earlier Christian ethicists talked about the proper function of human rights claims, I think it would be better if Christians only use the term "human rights" for what are often called "first-generation" rights. To say a government or military force has abused human rights is to say that a public organization has committed a serious act of injustice which will require serious believers to consider public protests and civil disobedience. This is very different from saying that a government should take steps to improve medical care, social security, or housing.

The so-called third-generation human rights include matters such as the right to political, economic, social, and cultural self-determination, the right to participate in and benefit from "the common heritage of mankind" (shared resources; scientific, technical, and other information and progress; and cultural traditions, sites, and monuments), and the right to social/economic development. Three more third-generation rights are the right to peace, the right to a healthy and sustainable

---

[65] It should be unnecessary to mention the way in which a society with a high level of human rights protection is a condition that allows many individuals and families to earn a sufficient income so that humanitarian aid is not needed. Justice provides a context within which both mercy and economic growth can flourish.

[66] I am thinking here of the studies of the Nobel Prize winner Amartya Sen, *Development as Freedom* (New York: Knopf, 1999).

environment, and the right to humanitarian disaster relief.[67] As with second-generation human rights, I would seriously question if it was *wise* to include all of these topics as human rights, as if they are equivalent in regard to basic justice as, e.g., freedom from slavery, freedom of speech, freedom of religion, freedom from arbitrary arrest and punishment.

Some of these third-generation rights are little more than explanations of what should be meant by some of the first-generation rights. For example, the right to participate in and benefit from the common heritage of mankind is little more than an explanation of the right to receive and impart information and ideas, already mentioned in Article 19 of the UN Declaration as a first-generation right. The right to economic development is little more than an explanation of the right to property, already mentioned in Article 17 of the UN Declaration. And as previously mentioned, the freedoms of speech and religion are what usually make effective humanitarian disaster relief possible; indeed, the practice of humanitarian aid for people in need is largely a part of the practice of religion for billions of people of various religions, including all Christians. If the first-generation rights are properly understood, then it is unnecessary to mention these additional rights; it may be unwise to mention them, because "if everything becomes a right, then nothing will be a right."

It is also unfortunate that the care of the environment has been described in human rights terms. God has given all people a responsibility, really a stewardship, to care for his creation. This is what we read in the report about the Garden of Eden. "The Lord God took the man and put him in the Garden of Eden to work it and take care of it." (Genesis 2:15) Destruction of the environment is a sin against this commandment of God. But not every moral responsibility should be described as a human right. Some of our duties to other people are better described as duties of mercy or duties of loyalty. And our care for the non-human creation is better described as a duty of stewardship of a treasure that has been entrusted to our care. People need an environment

---

[67] Most of the discussion of third-generation rights came after the UN Human Rights Declaration was already written, though this theme arises in some later human rights declarations. The only mention of a third-generation right in the 1948 declaration is the first part of article 27.

that is not too polluted, and we have a duty to care for God's world; why not simply say this instead of using confused language about a human right to a healthy and sustainable environment?

There is one additional problem with the third-generation rights. The supposed "right to political self-determination" can easily become an attempt to provide a deceptive moral defense for inhumane political movements. A twenty-first century follower of the Nazis could easily use this type of terminology to defend genocide, ethnic cleansing, or discrimination against some unpopular group in society; such policies could be defended as part of a nation's right to political self-determination. Of course, different countries and regions should be free to do some things differently than anyone else in the world, but this can easily become very ugly, really murderous, unless all the first- generation rights are firmly protected. And some political movements have argued that they want to implement third-generation rights before they fully protect first-generation rights: this is a formula for a human disaster.

4. How Do We Know?

We cannot avoid the question of how we know what rights people have. The answers one hears about what rights people have (and how we know what rights people have) seem to be partly dependent on one's theory about the origin of those rights. Thus, writers who think that rights come from the State or from society will be inclined to think people have whatever rights the state or society provides, which tends to lead to very short, limited lists of human rights. According to such theories, we know about these rights because they are publicly announced by law or a state declaration. Those writers who claim that rights come from the self tend to write as if we have as many rights as we want, which tends to lead to wildly exaggerated lists of supposed rights, lists that may resemble a child's Christmas wish list. We know we have these rights, according to these theories, by the very fact that we want these rights. Such opposing tendencies often make particular human rights claims sound arbitrary and therefore not worthy of serious consideration.

A truly serious way to consider what rights people have is to go back to the view of the person in classical Christian natural law theory, in which classical human rights theory is rooted. Thomas Aquinas and the other classical Christian ethicists saw the person as naturally living with a number of moral obligations which are rooted in the requirements of practical reason and everyday life. Because God created us in his image with certain responsibilities in his world, we have many duties, whether or not we always recognize these duties or recognize that these duties come from God. From this set of moral/religious facts, one can easily conclude that people have rights to do the things they are morally obligated to do. Our rights correspond to our moral duties. Specifically, people have a God-given moral obligation to speak, worship, assemble, work, raise a family, educate their children, and so on, leading to rights to do these things. These matters could be designated our "primary positive rights." In order to protect such primary rights, we need to have many specific legal arrangements and principles, matters such as fair trials and a principle like "innocent until proven guilty." These could be called procedural rights that protect primary and basic rights. And the term "basic rights" could be used to designate those things that are presupposed in our moral obligations, things such as rights to life, liberty, and the pursuit of happiness. Obviously, basic rights must be protected in order to allow people to exercise their primary positive rights. All of these little categories of rights are included in the normal lists of "first-generation" rights.

Some further illustrations may be in order. In the realm of work, the result of this type of human rights theory would be the following: Obviously, a wise government will follow well-considered economic policies that promote economic development and the availability of good jobs, but there is no basic injustice, no violation of human rights, unless government interferes with a person's moral obligation to work. A government has not committed injustice if some citizens do not succeed in finding exactly the jobs they desire. In the realm of education: Obviously, a stable government and healthy economy require a well-educated population, so the government has a legitimate interest in both elementary and higher education. But individuals, families, and local communities have strong obligations to speak their mind, practice their religion, and educate their children in light of their own convictions and beliefs. Thus, there is a violation of human rights if any government carries out its proper obligations in a manner that prevents individuals and families from carrying out their moral obligations. There is not a violation of human rights if the government does not provide all the education that might be desirable. In general, we should attempt to define the particular rights that people have in light of the normal obligations and responsibilities that people have because they live in God's world, created in his image.

5. Personal Comments

The biblical message should transform how we think and act in regard to human value, human dignity, and human rights. Because of creation, most people have some vague awareness of the value or dignity of human life; this is often joined with a vague awareness of moral obligations toward others. But sin easily turns an awareness of human dignity into pride, while also reducing our interest in any obligations toward other people. Remember the Chinese fishermen encountered by Hudson Taylor.

Many things should change when we hear, understand, and accept the biblical message. The gospel of Christ promises forgiveness of sins and peace with God by faith in Jesus Christ; the biblical message also contains important declarations about human dignity and the duties we have toward others. Without the biblical message, we would not appreciate the value of human life, nor would we be easily able to distinguish justice from mercy. These biblical truths should inform and transform the lives of Christians and our various churches and ministries. We need to be the people who declare the value of human life while we also embody that message in Christian communities that practice real mercy and promote real justice. Our hope should be that we not only bring honor to God by our lives and witness; our hope should be that we also influence our various cultures and become tools of both God's saving grace and his preserving grace.

Many people are not so extremely callous as the fishermen encountered by Hudson Taylor when his friend drowned. One of the reasons that not all are so callous is because they have been influenced by the biblical message, sometimes in a very indirect manner. So let us consider very seriously what we can do to increase both the direct and the indirect influence of that wonderful biblical message, to bring a little more justice and a little more mercy into a broken, needy world.

Appendix: The United Nations Universal Declaration of Human Rights

Preamble

Whereas recognition of the inherent dignity and of the equal and inalienable rights of all members of the human family is the foundation of freedom, justice and peace in the world,

Whereas disregard and contempt for human rights have resulted in barbarous acts which have outraged the conscience of mankind, and the advent of a world in which human beings shall enjoy freedom of speech and belief and freedom from fear and want has been proclaimed as the highest aspiration of the common people,

Whereas it is essential, if man is not to be compelled to have recourse, as a last resort, to rebellion against tyranny and oppression, that human rights should be protected by the rule of law,

Whereas it is essential to promote the development of friendly relations between nations,

Whereas the peoples of the United Nations have in the Charter reaffirmed their faith in fundamental human rights, in the dignity and worth of the human person and in the equal rights of men and women and have determined to promote social progress and better standards of life in larger freedom,

Whereas Member States have pledged themselves to achieve, in cooperation with the United Nations, the promotion of universal respect for and observance of human rights and fundamental freedoms,

Whereas a common understanding of these rights and freedoms is of the greatest importance for the full realization of this pledge,

Now, therefore,

THE GENERAL ASSEMBLY

Proclaims this Universal Declaration of Human Rights as a common standard of achievement for all peoples and all nations, to the end that every individual and every organ of society, keeping this Declaration constantly in mind, shall strive by teaching and education to promote respect for these rights and freedoms and by progressive measures, national and international, to secure their universal and effective recognition and observance, both among the peoples of Member States themselves and among the peoples of territories under their jurisdiction.

Article 1

All human beings are born free and equal in dignity and rights. They are endowed with reason and conscience and should act towards one another in a spirit of brotherhood.

Article 2

Everyone is entitled to all the rights and freedoms set forth in this Declaration, without distinction of any kind, such as race, color, sex, language, religion, political or other opinion, national or social origin, property, birth or other status.

Furthermore, no distinction shall be made on the basis of the political, jurisdictional or international status of the country or territory to which a person belongs, whether it be independent, trust, non-self-governing or under any other limitation of sovereignty.

Article 3

Everyone has the right to life, liberty, and the security of person.

Article 4

No one shall be held in slavery or servitude; slavery and the slave trade shall be prohibited in all their forms.

Article 5

No one shall be subjected to torture or to cruel, inhumane or degrading treatment or punishment.

Article 6

Everyone has a right to recognition everywhere as a person before the law.

Article 7

All are equal before the law and are entitled without any discrimination to equal protection of the law. All are entitled to equal protection against any discrimination in violation of this Declaration and against any incitement to such discrimination.

Article 8

Everyone has the right to an effective remedy by the competent national tribunals for acts violating the fundamental rights granted him by the constitution or by law.

Article 9

No one shall be subject to arbitrary arrest, detention, or exile.

Article 10

Everyone is entitled in full equality to a fair and public hearing by an independent and impartial tribunal, in the determination of his rights and obligation and of any criminal charge against him.

Article 11

1. Everyone charged with a penal offence has the right to be presumed innocent until proved guilty according to law in a public trial at which he has had all the guaranties necessary for his defense

2. No one shall be held guilty of any penal offence on account of any act or omission which did not constitute a penal offence, under national or international law, at the time when it was

committed. Nor shall a heavier penalty be imposed than the one that was applicable at the time the penal offence was committed.

Article 12

No one shall be subjected to arbitrary interference with his privacy, family, home, or correspondence, nor to attacks upon his honor and reputation. Everyone has the right to the protection of the law against such interference or attacks.

Article 13

1. Everyone has the right to freedom of movement and residence within the borders of each State.

2. Everyone has the right leave any country, including his own, and to return to his country.

Article 14

1. Everyone has the right to seek and to enjoy on other countries asylum from persecution.

2. This right may not be invoked in the case of prosecutions genuinely arising from nonpolitical crimes or from acts contrary to the purposes and principles of the United Nations.

Article 15

1. Everyone has a right to a nationality.

2. No one shall be arbitrarily deprived of his nationality nor denied the right to change his nationality.

Article 16

1. Men and women of full age, without any limitation due to race, nationality or religion, have the right to marry and to found a family. They are entitled to equal rights as to marriage, during marriage and at its dissolution.

2. Marriage shall be entered into only with the free and full consent of the intending spouses.

3. The family is the natural and fundamental group unit of society and is entitled to protection by society and the State.

Article 17

1. Everyone has the right to own property alone as well as in association with others.

2. No one shall be arbitrarily deprived of his property.

Article 18

Everyone has the right to freedom of thought, conscience and religion; this right includes freedom to change his religion or belief, and freedom, either alone or in community with others and in public or private, to manifest his religion or belief in teaching, practice, worship and observance.

Article 19

Everyone has the right to freedom of opinion and expression; this right includes freedom to hold opinions without interference and to seek, receive and impart information and ideas through any media and regardless of frontiers.

Article 20

1. Everyone has the right to freedom of peaceful assembly and association.

2. No one may be compelled to belong to an association.

Article 21

1. Everyone has the right to take part in the government of his country, directly or through freely chosen representatives.

2. Everyone has the right of equal access to public service in his country.

3. The will of the people shall be the basis of the authority of government; this will shall be expressed in periodic and genuine elections which shall be by universal and equal suffrage and shall be held by secret vote or by equivalent free voting procedures.

Article 22

Everyone, as a member of society, has the right to social security and is entitled to realization, through national effort and international co-operation and in accordance with the organization and resources of each State, of the economic, social and cultural rights indispensable for his dignity and the free development of his personality.

Article 23

1. Everyone has the right to work, to free choice of employment, to just and favorable conditions of work and to protection against unemployment.

2. Everyone, without any discrimination, has the right to equal pay for equal work.

3. Everyone who works has the right to just and favorable remuneration ensuring for himself and his family an existence worthy of human dignity, and supplemented, if necessary, by other means of social protection.

4. Everyone has the right to form and to join trade unions for the protection of his interests.

Article 24

Everyone has the right to rest and leisure, including reasonable limitation of working hours and periodic holidays with pay.

Article 25

1. Everyone has the right to a standard of living adequate for the health and well-being of himself and of his family, including food, clothing, housing and medical care and necessary social services, and the right to security in the event of unemployment, sickness, disability, widowhood, old age or other lack of livelihood in circumstances beyond his control.

2. Motherhood and childhood are entitled to special care and assistance. All children, whether born in or out of wedlock, shall enjoy the same social protection.

Article 26

1. Everyone has the right to education. Education shall be free, at least in the elementary and fundamental stages. Elementary education shall be compulsory. Technical and professional education shall be made generally available and higher education shall be equally accessible to all on the basis of merit.

2. Education shall be directed to the full development of the human personality and to the strengthening of respect for human rights and fundamental freedoms. It shall promote understanding, tolerance and friendship among all nations, racial or religious groups, and shall further the activities of the United Nations for the maintenance of peace.

3. Parents have a prior right to choose the kind of education that shall be given to their children.

Article 27

1. Everyone has the right freely to participate in the cultural life of the community, to enjoy the arts and to share in scientific advancement and its benefits.

2. Everyone has the right to the protection of the moral and material interests resulting from any scientific, literary or artistic production of which he is the author.

Article 28

Everyone is entitled to a social and international order in which the rights and freedoms set forth in this Declaration can be fully realized.

Article 29

1. Everyone has duties to the community in which alone the free and full development of his personality is possible.

2. In the exercise of his rights and freedoms, everyone shall be subject only to such limitations as are determined by law solely for the purpose of securing due recognition and respect for the rights and freedoms of others and of meeting the just requirements of morality, public order and the general welfare in a democratic society.

3. These rights and freedoms may in no case be exercised contrary to the purposes and principles of the United Nations.

Article 30

Nothing in this Declaration may be interpreted as implying for any State, group or person any right to engage in any activity or to perform any act aimed at the destruction of any of the rights and freedoms set forth herein.

PROTECTING HUMAN RIGHTS IN PRACTICE

In spite of all the violence and suffering in the world, our world would be far worse without the many contributions of Christians and the influence of biblical ideas. From the earliest days of the Christian church, believers learned the new commandment that Jesus gave us: "Love one another. As I have loved you, so you must love one another. By this will all men know that you are my disciples, if you love one another." (John 13:34-35) This commandment began to change the way Christians treated each other, so they (really we) began to care for our sick, our elderly, our poor, our dying, our prisoners, our persecuted. And this care could not be artificially limited to believers; it very properly began to be extended to wider groups of people as an extension of the love of Jesus for all. Within the first generation of the church, the apostle Paul clarified the complementary relationship between love for believers and love for all our neighbors. "Therefore, as we have opportunity, let us do good to all people, especially to those who belong to the family of believers." (Galatians 6:10)

At first, in Christian history, believers especially invested much of their very limited time and energy into caring for the weak and helpless. They buried the dead who would not otherwise have a dignified burial. They took care of orphans, many of whom were unwanted babies who had been abandoned by their parents. And when one Christian was a slave owned by another Christian, they even asked that the whole relationship be substantially changed. (See the New Testament book of Philemon.) These actions, joined with the explanation of these actions, stood as a living rebuke and prophetic confrontation with the cruelty of the surrounding culture. And slowly the believers began to contribute ideas, better customs, humane ways of life, and whole institutions (such as hospitals, orphanages, and schools) to the surrounding world. Some of these have become standard practice in the world without many people noticing why we do these things or where the motivation originated. For example, in much of the world today, people know they should get out of the way when an ambulance comes down the street with flashing lights and a screaming siren; I think this very good practice is partly the result of the contributions of Christians and biblical ideas for many centuries. Ancient Roman culture would probably have not been so concerned with human suffering.

It seems to have been somewhat later in Christian history that believers started to become extensively involved in protecting justice for people who were being denied justice. The first generations of Christians were mostly very poor and socially marginalized, without ready access to public opinion or government; this situation almost forced the early Christians to a limited practice of mercy without being able to contribute much to the public practice of justice. By the nineteenth century, however, we have outstanding examples of evangelical Christians who were extensively and sacrificially involved in trying to help protect the rights of other people. Evangelical Christians were very active in trying to protect the rights of the people who were held in slavery (especially in Great Britain and North America), as well as in arguing for freedom of religion (for all religions) in the Ottoman Empire (partly today's Turkey). Evangelical Christians have a heritage of not only practicing personal love and mercy but also establishing organizations and programs to provide mercy and promote public justice (human rights protection).

If you have read this little book this far, you are probably interested in what you can do to increase and improve the contributions of Christians to protecting human rights. Here are my suggestions of steps many can take.

1. Publicize Human Rights Abuses.

There is almost always real suffering when someone's God-given rights are abused. Most other people will have a God-given sympathy response when they hear the stories or see pictures of people who are suffering. And if that suffering is caused by human cruelty or by an evil government, powerful anger at those committing injustice will strengthen the sympathy response. Sympathy for those getting hurt and anger against those hurting others can stimulate a wide range of action. Some will demand that the criminals against humanity be called to account in a court, while others will take steps to help the wounded. One of the best steps we can take when human rights are being harmed is to tell the stories and show the pictures of the victims. This can reduce the problem now and change what people will do in the future. And people who are hurting others usually know that many people around the world will become angry at them; they may even have a feeling inside that what they are doing is deeply wrong. Publicity is a first step toward reducing human rights abuses.

Probably only a few readers are called to become journalists, but in the twenty-first century, many of us can assist in the process of confronting human rights abuses by means of communicating. Whenever there are human rights abuses occurring, Christians should make their best effort to bring the problem to the attention of many other people by means of carefully reporting or sending pictures of what is happening. This might be only by word of mouth if one has limited means of communication. Or it might be by sending reports to newspapers, television stations, or websites. In some situations, the best thing to do may be to communicate within the resources of our churches and mission agencies, many of which have newsletters, websites, or other means of communication. Publicity will almost always help reduce the pressure on people who are persecuted for their faith, who are denied basic freedoms, or who are threatened with ethnic cleansing or genocide. Many Christians will be able to help publicize such problems. And we should help *whenever we can*. Freedom of speech and freedom of the media have some times become established, legally protected practices because Christians have decided they need to obey a God-given duty to speak freely about human suffering; we must speak openly and freely whenever we know that people who are created in the image of God are being unnecessarily hurt.

2. Teach and Preach the Whole Message of God.

Of course, all Christians in positions of teaching and preaching in our churches and other ministries will want to "proclaim the whole will of God" as Paul described his task. (Acts 20:27) The center of evangelical proclamation and teaching should always be the gospel of the death and resurrection of Christ, along with the proper responses of repentance, faith, gratitude, and new obedience. But the center of our preaching is not the whole story or the whole Word of God. Like the prophet Amos of the Old Testament (Read Amos chapters 1 and 2 if his preaching is not vivid in your memory.), our preachers and teachers should look for the right occasions to confront the great sins against humanity in our time. Amos was God's spokesman in his time; that task falls to preachers and Christian teachers today. This may require great courage, but it is part of the calling of Christian leaders. Properly prophetic preaching which declares God's displeasure at crimes against humanity will empower the entire Body of Christ to join in publicizing human rights abuses. We must be very careful not to confuse our preaching of God's Word with our political preferences; we must also be careful not to lose our courage to proclaim God's wrath when his image in human beings is attacked.

A further part of the full message of God is how we should understand what a human being is. It is worth repeating: many people in the world today have no clear answers to the questions about what a human being is. We have biblical answers that can sometimes be largely accepted by many people before they come to faith. And these biblical answers can make a huge contribution to a humane way of life, whether or not our neighbors come to faith in Christ. As I would explain the biblical teaching, there are two sides to human nature; we have great dignity and worth because we are created in the image of God; we also have the potential to become murderers because sin lies deep within the human heart. Human beings are worth protecting because they are made in the image of God; they sometimes need to be restrained because of sin. This two-sided understanding of human nature should be widely taught and discussed among evangelical Christians and offered as an answer to all those who have questions about what it means to be human. We should try to help this description of humans to slowly slide into the rest of our world, where this way of thinking can lead to healthier communities and a more humane way of life. Ideas have consequences, and good ideas have good consequences.

3. Here Are Some Occasional Steps.

There are several other steps that a few Christians may be able to take if the proper occasion arises. Only a small number of believers will be in positions in which they can make these changes, but all well-educated believers should be aware of these matters.

1. There is generally a much higher level of protection for human rights if a state or country has a system of courts and professional judges that is largely independent of the administration (president or prime minister) of the country. Whenever there are major political changes, we should encourage the establishment of an independent court system.

2. Written codes of human rights can make a significant contribution, especially if these codes or declarations are discussed repeatedly. Of course, just the official proclamation of human rights does not lead to any automatic protection of real human beings, but such declarations and codes set a public, official standard that can begin to contribute to justice in practice.

3. We should call on governments and all military forces to follow the human rights declarations and codes which they have often affirmed or signed but which they may have forgotten. Many countries have signed very good human rights documents which must now be followed; someone must call on government to follow the standards they have publicly affirmed.

4. A written constitution which is carefully followed usually helps protect the rights of people in that country or state. In times of national transition, we should encourage the careful writing of constitutions which include human rights protections.

5. Strong families and strong churches will, with time, tend to hold governments and military/police forces in some restraint and to prevent some serious abuses. In some circumstances, courageous churches can serve as a balance of power when a government starts moving in an inhumane or unjust direction.

6. Chaos and massive corruption can easily threaten the lives of people as much as inhumane totalitarian governments. Just government that protects the lives and rights of people is the antidote to both chaos and inhumane government.

7. Christians should always be willing to consider public protests and even non-violent civil disobedience to protect the rights of people, but these actions must be very carefully and cautiously considered. We should be very cautious about ever doing anything that might cause the collapse of public order, since the resulting chaos could easily be worse than a harsh government.

8. Caring for the victims of human rights abuses is one of the most effective public rebukes of those who committed the crimes. We must become leaders in caring for the victims of crimes against humanity.

4. This Is My Personal Plea.

I would appeal to you, my fellow evangelical Christians, to make the protection of human rights an important part of your understanding of Christian ethics, an important part of your response to God's undeserved grace in Christ. There have been far too many holocausts in our world. But courageous, God-fearing people can make a difference. Many millions of people today call themselves Christians. If even a small number of us do what we can to protect the rights of our neighbors, the world will be a much better place. **And God will be glorified.**

Of course, my plea is very big. It will require learning to speak the language of human rights, an important contemporary language about public justice, a language which has sometimes been used to communicate foolish ideas. But as believers we should think big for the glory of God, while we also learn and work diligently at the immediately possible steps. As a good friend has said,

> Where would our world be if no one had ever demanded changes that seemed, at the moment, to be totally unimaginable? But also: Where would our world be, if we only talked about the big matters that we cannot change right now and did not make use of the possibilities that appear right now?[68]

I would like us to try to change our world for Jesus.

---

[68] Thomas Schirrmacher, *Ethik,* Volume 3, p. 553.

ABOUT THE AUTHOR

Prof. Th. Johnson received his Ph.D. in ethics and philosophical theology within an interdisciplinary religion and humanities program from the University of Iowa (1987) after spending a year as a research scholar at Eberhard Karls Universität (Tübingen, Germany) sponsored by the German Academic Exchange Service, the German equivalent of a Fulbright fellowship. His university studies included the equivalents of non-thesis MA degrees (1983) in three fields: History of Christianity, Comparative Theology and Ethics (Jewish, Protestant, and Catholic) and Psychology of Religion. His previous education included an Advanced CPE certificate from Missouri Baptist Hospital (St. Louis, 1981), a Master of Divinity (Magna Cum Laude) from Covenant Theological Seminary (St. Louis, 1981), a BA (Cum Laude) from Hope College (Michigan, 1977), and studies at a Teen Challenge Bible Institute (Nieder-Wöllstadt, Germany, 1973). He is an ordained minister of the Presbyterian Church in America and was founding pastor of Hope Evangelical Church in Iowa City, Iowa. In the 1980s he was an academic assistant to the well-known theologian Donald Bloesch; in the early 90s he worked as a writer/research for Chuck Colson. Dr. Johnson served as an adjunct professor of philosophy at Kirkwood Community College in Iowa, 1991-1994, and as a Visiting Professor at the European Humanities University in Minsk, Belarus, 1994-1996. UHU was a dissident, anti-Communist university which was closed by force at the orders of the Belarusian dictator in 2004.

In 1996, Thomas, Leslie and their children (Justin, Heather and Aimee) relocated to Prague. Dr. Johnson taught numerous classes in ethics and philosophy of religion at Anglo-American University (1996-2000) and historic Charles University (1998-2006). Since 2003 he has been Professor of Apologetics and Ethics for Martin Bucer Seminary (MBS) which has several study centers in major German cities, as well as in Austria and Switzerland, and in both Ankara and Istanbul, Turkey; in 2004 he helped establish the MBS study center in Zlin, Czech Republic. In 2007 he was also appointed MBS Vice President for Research and Personnel Development, to coordinate research, publications, and the development of new evangelical scholars for central Europe. Temporarily he is assisting Baltic Reformed Theological Seminary (Riga, Latvia and Vilnius, Lithuania) as interim dean, while they are moving into a new phase of their work which may include founding a series of Christian Studies programs in a Lithuanian university. Since 2004 he has been directing the Comenius Institute (Prague), with several projects which seek to develop a new evangelical academic witness. His major theoretical book, Natural Law Ethics: An Evangelical Proposal (Bonn: VKW, 2005) is part of his personal response to secularism in Western culture. His forthcoming book on the Trinity attempts to understand all of life in light of a Christian understanding of God, a protest against the trend to understand God in light of our secular lives; his forthcoming book on Human Rights illustrates an approach to social ethics inspired by the ideas of Francis Schaeffer, C. S. Lewis, and Helmut Thielicke. He regards knowledge and education as having as much to do with perspective as with information, an approach which has allowed him to teach university level courses in diverse fields including Business Ethics, Medical Ethics, Political Ethics, Religion and Literature, Religion and Society, Psychology of Religion, as well as a wide range of courses in philosophy, theology, and religious history. He has lectured in eleven countries and has about 80 published articles, essays, and reviews in several languages. Since 1994 his work has been largely sponsored through the International Institute for Christian Studies.

Leslie served in a wide variety of roles in primary and secondary education in Prague, before being appointed as the first principal and now director of the Christian International School of Prague (CISP), a new English language school for missionaries, Czechs, and other internationals. Classes began in September 2004. After beginning with 10 students, CISP reached 85 students in September 2008. Leslie graduated from Covenant College in the USA in May 2005 with an M.Ed. in integrated curriculum design. Justin graduated from Covenant College in 2003, and currently works as a military legislative assistant for Congressman (R) Todd Akin in Washington, DC. Heather graduated from Covenant College in 2005 and moved to St. Louis, Missouri, where she is currently a case worker for St. Louis social services. Justin was married (to Erika Ridgeway) in the spring of 2007, and Heather was married (to Lloyd Jackson) in the summer of 2007. Aimee graduated from CISP and began her studies at Wheaton College in the fall of 2008.

World Evangelical Alliance

World Evangelical Alliance is a global ministry working with local churches around the world to join in common concern to live and proclaim the Good News of Jesus in their communities. WEA is a network of churches in 128 nations that have each formed an evangelical alliance and over 100 international organizations joining together to give a worldwide identity, voice and platform to more than 420 million evangelical Christians. Seeking holiness, justice and renewal at every level of society – individual, family, community and culture, God is glorified and the nations of the earth are forever transformed.

Christians from ten countries met in London in 1846 for the purpose of launching, in their own words, "a new thing in church history, a definite organization for the expression of unity amongst Christian individuals belonging to different churches." This was the beginning of a vision that was fulfilled in 1951 when believers from 21 countries officially formed the World Evangelical Fellowship. Today, 150 years after the London gathering, WEA is a dynamic global structure for unity and action that embraces 420 million evangelicals in 128 countries. It is a unity based on the historic Christian faith expressed in the evangelical tradition. And it looks to the future with vision to accomplish God's purposes in discipling the nations for Jesus Christ.

Today, WEA seeks to strengthen local churches through national alliances, supporting and coordinating grassroots leadership and seeking practical ways of showing the unity of the body of Christ.

Commissions:

- Missions
- Religious Liberty
- Women's Concerns
- Theology
- Youth
- Information Technology

Suite 1153, 13351 Commerce Parkway
Richmond, BC. V6V 2X7 Canada
Phone +1 / 604-214-8620
Fax +1 / 604-214-8621
www.worldevangelicals.org

International Institute for Religious Freedom

The "International Institute for Religious Freedom" (IIRF) is a network of professors, researchers, academics and specialists from all continents, which work on reliable data on the violation of religious freedom worldwide and are interested in adding this topic to college and university programmes, especially in the areas of law, sociology, religious studies and theological programmes.

Task

While numerous other organizations such as human rights groups, mission boards and the Religious Liberty Commission (RLC) of the World Evangelical Alliance plus several active RLCs of regional and national alliances provide relevant information and prayer requests or assist on the scene, this institute aims to work on a long-term basis and to insure that comprehensive studies are carried out and made available.

Rather than duplicating existing projects, the International Institute for Religious Freedom intends to organize new projects or make information on existing projects more available. Our fields include:

- the publication of long-term, citable literature (such as books, annuals, journals and legal documentations);
- Suggestions for teaching and study at Christian universities, seminaries and Bible colleges all over the world;
- Groundwork studies into the legal aspects (such as official legal background in various nations, historical studies, certification of court cases);
- Theological studies (for example, the ethics of human rights, theology of persecution, the history of persecution);
- Introduction of such subjects into theological training (in literature, seminars, courses of study, networking between seminaries, direction of academic papers such as dissertations)
- Long-term: an international archive or a network of existing archives.

Online / Contact

- www.iirf.eu / info@iirf.eu

Martin Bucer Seminary

Faithful to biblical truth
Cooperating with the Evangelical Alliance
Reformed

MARTIN
BUCER
SEMINAR

Solid training for the Kingdom of God

- Alternative theological education
- Study while serving a church or working another job
- Enables students to remain in their own churches
- Encourages independent thinking
- Learning from the growth of the universal church.

Academic

- For the Bachelor's degree: 180 Bologna-Credits
- For the Master's degree: 120 additional Credits
- Both old and new teaching methods: All day seminars, independent study, term papers, etc.

Our Orientation:

- Complete trust in the reliability of the Bible
- Building on reformation theology
- Based on the confession of the German Evangelical Alliance
- Open for innovations in the Kingdom of God

Our Emphasis:

- The Bible
- Ethics and Basic Theology
- Missions
- The Church

Our Style:

- Innovative
- Relevant to society
- International
- Research oriented
- Interdisciplinary

Structure

- 11 study centers in 5 countries with local partners
- 5 research institutes
- Rector: Prof. Dr. Thomas Schirrmacher
- Deans: Thomas Kinker, Th.D.; Titus Vogt, lic. theol.

Missions through research

- Institute for Religious Freedom
- Institute for Islamic Studies
- Institute for Life and Family Studies
- Institute for Crisis, Dying, and Grief Counseling
- Institute for Pastoral Care

www.bucer.eu • info@bucer.eu

Berlin | Bonn | Chemnitz Hamburg Pforzheim

Ankara Innsbruck Istanbul Prague Zlin Zurich

Giving Hands

GIVING HANDS GERMANY (GH) was established in 1995 and is officially recognized as a nonprofit foreign aid organization. It is an international operating charity that – up to now – has been supporting projects in about 40 countries on four continents. In particular we care for orphans and street children. Our major focus is on Africa and Central America. GIVING HANDS always mainly provides assistance for self-help.

The charity itself is not bound to any church, but on the spot we are co-operating with churches of all denominations. Naturally we also cooperate with other charities as well as governmental organizations to provide assistance as effective as possible under the given circumstances.

The work of GIVING HANDS GERMANY is controlled by a supervisory board. Members of this board are Dr. theol. Thomas Schirrmacher (chairman), Colonel V. Doner and Kathleen McCall. Dr. Christine Schirrmacher is registered as legal manager of GIVING HANDS at the local district court. The local office and work of the charity are coordinated by Rev. Horst J. Kreie as executive manager.

Thanks to our international contacts companies and organizations from many countries time and again provide containers with gifts in kind which we send to the different destinations where these goods help to satisfy elementary needs. This statutory purpose is put into practice by granting nutrition, clothing, education, construction and maintenance of training centers at home and abroad, construction of wells and operation of water treatment systems, guidance for self-help and transportation of goods and gifts to areas and countries where needy people live.

These aims are aspired to the glory of the Lord according to the basic Christian principles put down in the Holy Bible.

Adenauerallee 11 · D-53111 Bonn · Germany
Phone: +49 / 228 / 695531 · Fax +49 / 228 / 695532
www.gebende-haende.de · info@gebende-haende.de